THERE IS GOING TO BE BLOODSHED!

I grabbed Hiers' gun with both hands and drew it away from my body (for the pistol would probably go off and the family jewels - or other vital organs - would suffer the consequences). After a short struggle, the gun hit the floor, and I hit Hiers as hard as I could. I saw his eyes roll in their sockets, but he didn't go down. So, I slugged him again, and he finally sank to the kitchen floor.

THIS BOOK IS DEDICATED TO ALL THE BRAVE LAW ENFORCEMENT MEN AND WOMEN WHO GAVE THEIR LIVES IN THE LINE OF DUTY.

I would personally like to honor:

Lieutenant William J. Taylor, Mansfield, Ohio Police Department. Shot to death while responding to a domestic quarrel. 1948

Patrolman Robert E. Karsmizki, Ohio State Highway Patrol. Shot to death while attempting to apprehend a subject in a stolen car.   1957

Police Officer Michael Hutchinson, Mansfield, Ohio Police Department. Shot to death investigating an armed robbery.   1976

Deputy Michael Yahl, Lee County Sheriff's Department, Florida. Shot to death responding to an armored car robbery.   1976

Deputy Lynn Hall, Lee County Sheriff's Department, Florida. Shot to death while attempting to apprehend a subject in a stolen car.   1979

Assistant State Attorney Eugene Barry, 20th Judicial District, Florida. Shot to death following a narcotics prosecution.   1982

POLICING PARADISE
SANIBEL ISLAND

by
John P. Butler
Chief of Police (Ret.)
with
Margaret H. Greenberg

SANIBEL ISLAND

ISBN 0-930942-18-3
Library of Congress Catalog Card Number 91-092131

Printed in the United States of America by:
Sutherland Printing Company, Inc.
Hwy 63 North
Montezuma, IA 50171

TABLE OF CONTENTS

PROLOGUE

A small spit of sand that emerged from the sea around 3,000 B.C., Sanibel is little more than a spot on the map off the southwest coast of Florida. Only twelve miles long and barely two miles wide, the island's promoters describe "the Tahiti of the United States" as a tropical paradise blessed with balmy breezes, towering palm trees, and miles of immaculate beaches. A sun-drenched refuge where people can escape the pressures of civilization without giving up any of its amenities, Sanibel is the perfect vacation playground.

In the early seventies, appalled by Lee County's proposals for massive development on their sanctuary island, a majority of Sanibel's citizens decided that the best way to fight the county was to become a city. Since the incorporation of a barrier island with only 2,500 residents was the kind of David vs. Goliath story that appealed to the press, Sanibel made national headlines.

"Paradise Fights Back" in *Sports Illustrated*, and the Chicago *Tribune*'s "Conflict in Paradise," were typical of the articles that appeared in major publications. The little seashell island would solve all its problems by creating a comprehensive land use plan designed to limit growth and keep greedy developers at bay. Subsequently, Sanibel's "CLUP" was hailed as a model for conservation efforts throughout the nation.

Fortunately, criminal activity wasn't a major problem when Sanibel incorporated in 1974. For in those days, "the shellers went to bed at eight and the hellers went to bed at nine." However, the handwriting was on the wall in the form of traffic counts that revealed an astronomical increase in the number of cars pouring across the causeway. As a result, residents had good reason to be concerned about an influx of "undesirables." But above all, nobody could do anything about the incredible traffic congestion during the tourist season. Thus, when Sanibel's first council met in December of 1974, establishing a police department was very high on their list of priorities.

Whether by fate or coincidence, Sanibel incorporated the same year I retired as the Chief of the Mansfield Police Department in Ohio. After twenty-six years as a professional police officer in an industrial city, I looked forward to leading a less stressful life. Not surprisingly, so did my wife. Thus, when Betty wanted to move to Fort Myers Beach, where we had previously vacationed, I readily agreed.

For several months, Betty and I enjoyed the good life on "the beach." Our neighbors couldn't have been more friendly, and we were invited to countless parties where the booze flowed freely. When not partying, or recuperating from partying, I went fishing.

But since a life devoted to socializing and fishing was neither purposeful nor challenging, I soon became bored out of my gourd - and undoubtedly a nuisance around the house. Therefore, when I heard that Sanibel was looking for someone to organize a police department and serve as its chief, I applied for the position and was interviewed by Councilwoman Zelda "Zee" Butler (no relation, despite persistent rumors to the contrary).

Formerly a leading proponent of incorporation, Zee was a highly attractive, intelligent, and articulate woman. Smart enough to realize that she knew nothing about police work, but everything about Sanibel's $250,000 budget, Zee concentrated on the latter during our interview. Specifically, how did I propose to spend the $80,000 earmarked for the police department?

Although Zelda probably posed the same question to some two dozen other applicants, she must have preferred my answer to theirs. For in February of 1975, just three months after incorporation, the city council announced my appointment as Chief of the Sanibel Police Department (SPD).

Following a standing ovation and filled with enthusiasm, I went to the SPD's headquarters: a small room in the Periwinkle Place shopping center.

* * *

During the next few months, I hired a secretary, three officers, two dispatchers, and blew the rest of my budget on the SPD's first patrol vehicle. This four-wheel drive assisted us in handling a great many of the calls we received involving incidents that happened on the beach.

While Sanibel's world-famous shelling beaches attract hordes of people, not all go there to collect seashells. As a result, the SPD received numerous complaints about nudists, male exhibitionists and, above all, break-ins at the public beach accesses where "day trippers" parked their cars.

But in addition to responding to complaints about some of the people who went to the beach, the SPD dealt with calls concerning items that washed up on it. While crab traps, dead loggerhead turtles, and mounds of malodorous fish killed by red tide constituted harmless debris, the sea occasionally deposited potentially dangerous objects.

Chief among them were bombs and machine-gun bullets dating from World War II, for the Air Corps had practiced bombing and strafing near Sanibel's then-deserted beaches. Moreover, when the SPD was still in its infancy and ill-equipped to deal with them, several tons of marijuana landed on the Sanibel and Captiva beaches.

But during the twelve-and-a-half years I served as Chief of the SPD, a badly decomposed body was by far the most dreadful thing that washed up on the beach.

GETTING AWAY WITH MURDER

In the early morning of March 6, 1979, construction workers at the Casa Ybel resort on the Gulf of Mexico reported a dead body floating along the shore. Given the serious nature of the call, our officers soon appeared upon the scene. But one look at the gruesome corpse was enough to make all of us wish we'd been off duty when the call came in.

Except for a weight belt around the waist, the body was completely naked. Crabs and other sea creatures had eaten all the flesh and internal organs, a clear indication that the corpse had been in the water for some time. The skull was bald, the body devoid of hair, and the remaining skin hung loosely around the bones.

Given the advanced state of decomposition, it was impossible to tell whether the human skeleton was male or female. It was also impossible to tell whether the individual had been the victim of an unfortunate scuba-diving accident or the victim of foul play. But in such situations, it's not up to the police to make those determinations. Rather, our job is to call the Medical Examiner and protect the body until he arrives.

Had it not been for the construction workers at Casa Ybel, protecting what little remained of the corpse would have been highly problematical. For the body was constantly buffeted by an incoming tide, and we desperately needed something fairly sturdy to shield it. The workers immediately volunteered to bring down pieces of plywood, which enabled us to contain the remains.

Since the month of March marks the height of the winter tourist season on Sanibel, shellers soon swarmed all over the beach. Naturally, many stopped to examine what we had found. But when they saw a decomposed corpse rather than a rare shell, they quickly backed away and maintained a respectful silence.

Much to my relief, Dr. Wallace Graves, the M.E., soon arrived by helicopter and took charge of the corpse. The latter was carefully placed on a piece of plywood, and the chopper subsequently transported both the mortal remains and the Medical Examiner to Fort Myers. Realizing that time was of the essence, Dr. Graves immediately performed an autopsy and reported the results.

The deceased was a white female in her mid-twenties, and her body had been in the water four to five weeks. The cause of death was bludgeoning, not drowning. Moreover, Dr. Graves had discovered and removed a gold ring firmly imbedded in one of the victim's fingers, an indication that she had instinctively thrown up her hands in a vain attempt to ward off blows to the head. Unfortunately, someone had wielded a blunt object with sufficient force to kill her - and ram the ring into her finger.

Thanks to Dr. Graves' detailed autopsy report, the SPD now knew that the body on the beach was that of a woman who had been brutally murdered about a month ago and dumped into the Gulf of Mexico. But since we didn't know who she was, we had no idea who might have killed her. The gold ring constituted the only clue to her identity.

* * *

We immediately contacted all local news media and asked them to publicize the disappearance of a young, white female during the past month and include a description of the ring. As a result, the SPD soon received a dozen calls concerning young, white women who had recently disappeared. However, one caller, who saw the ring on TV, said that it belonged to her friend, Shirley Rhodes.

Of course, positive identification of the ring didn't constitute identification of the unrecognizable body. Moreover, no one had filed a missing-person report on Shirley Rhodes. Thus, we asked the caller to tell us everything she knew about her friend, and learned that - before moving to Fort Myers - Shirley had lived in Prince George's County, MD.

Armed with this information, the SPD contacted the Prince George's County P.D., and were fortunate to have an extremely hard-working detective assigned to assist us. Indeed, Detective Daniel Statkus left no stone unturned.

He interviewed people who knew Shirley Rhodes, took their statements, and persuaded Shirley's former dentist to open his office after hours and provide her dental records. Shortly thereafter, Eastern Airlines flew the records to Fort Myers, at no charge.

With the dental charts in hand, Dr. Graves soon identified the body - thereby confirming the worst fears of Shirley's friend. However, the SPD now faced the almost impossible task of finding out who had killed Shirley Rhodes and thrown her body into the sea. For in this particular case, the perpetrator stood an excellent chance of getting away with murder for several reasons.

Foremost among them was the fact that the crime had been committed over a month ago. Since the trail runs cold after forty-eight hours have passed, murders that are not solved during that limited period frequently remain unsolved. Furthermore, Shirley's killer had taken the trouble to place a weight belt around her waist. By the time her body rose to the surface, if indeed it ever did, nobody would be able to identify it.

But while the killer was careful about disposing of the body, he made no attempt to remove incriminating evidence from the actual scene of the crime. Thus, when members of the SPD and the Lee County Sheriff's Department (LCSD) went to Shirley's home in Lee County, they found her blood splattered all over the place - and her husband long gone.

Since it was now clearly established that the crime had occurred outside the jurisdiction of the SPD, the LCSD immediately took over the investigation. Thus, just three days after Shirley's body washed up on the beach, an arrest warrant was issued charging Alan Rhodes with first-degree murder.

Had it not been for the outstanding cooperation of various

governmental agencies, the news media and private citizens, the police would never have solved the crime in fifty-one hours. In fact, we might never have solved it. However, the case is by no means closed, for Alan Rhodes has been at large since 1979.

Given the passage of time, Rhodes will probably continue to remain at large - unless this heinous crime is publicized on television. Programs like *Unsolved Mysteries* and *America's Most Wanted* do an excellent job of recreating real crimes for their millions of viewers, and calls from the latter have led to the arrest of numerous perpetrators.

Thus, should a dramatization of the brutal slaying of Shirley Rhodes ever appear on national TV, the chances are good that Alan Rhodes will be arrested.

Office of the Sheriff

John J. McDougall

State of Florida
County of Lee

January 30th, 1991

John P. Butler, Chief (Ret.)
1525 San Carlos Bay Drive
Sanibel, Florida 33957

Dear Chief Butler:

Thank you for sending the chapter of your book concerning the Shirley Rhodes homicide. I have reviewed it. The facts seem accurate, and the sequence of events read well.

Continued success with this project. Enclosed is the picture of, Allan Rhodes as requested. I sincerely hope the arrest of Allan Rhodes will be the final chapter.

Good luck,

Richard Chard, Lieutenant
Lee County Sheriff's Office
Major Crimes Division

WANTED BY
LEE CO. SHERIFF'S DEPT.

HOMICIDE

ALAN JEFFREY RHODES
W/M   D.O.B.   7-9-54

HEIGHT	5'9"
WEIGHT	155
EYES	BROWN
HAIR	BROWN

A SPOOL OF THREAD

A robber who wears a mask and carries a gun assumes that the people that he plans to rob will be suitably impressed. In fact, he expects his victims to be so terrified that they'll gladly give him everything they own in exchange for their lives. As a rule, such is indeed the case. However, and much to the surprise of one armed robber in Mansfield, Ohio, there are exceptions to every rule.

Wearing a mask, a cowboy hat, and a crazy-looking jacket, the gun-toting bandit in question burst into Miller's bar around 1:00 A.M. and shouted, "This is a stickup!" But since the bartender and his half-dozen customers were all three sheets to the wind, this announcement failed to produce the desired effect. Instead, the besotted bartender ordered the robber to, "Get the fuck out of here!"

"Hey, I ain't kiddin'," protested the robber. "This *is* a stickup!" The drunken customers responded to that clarification by telling the yo-yo in the cowboy hat to get the hell out of there. Not knowing how to deal with a bunch of lushes who refused to take him seriously, the would-be robber fled the premises.

Unfortunately, the masked man who walked into the Casa Del Mama restaurant knew what to do when Julia Marabetti failed to take him seriously. As a result, this man made history by committing the first reported armed robbery in the City of Sanibel. But a spool of thread put an end to his enjoyment of that dubious distinction.

* * *

Named in honor of Julia Marabetti, the owner's mother, Casa Del Mama (now the Quarterdeck), was located a few hundred yards from the Bank of the Islands (now C & S Bank), on Periwinkle Way. A highly popular place for Sanibelians who liked to go out for breakfast, Casa Del Mama also appealed to people who wanted to have lunch or dinner in a friendly, family-type restaurant that didn't charge a fortune for the privilege of eating while ignoring the cheap pictures on the walls.

At 9:00 P.M. on February 9, 1976, it was business as usual at Casa Del Mama. Julia bustled about the kitchen, husband Sam socialized with some of the regular customers, and daughter-in-law Judy operated the cash register by the door where people paid on their way out. Like most island restaurants in those days, Casa Del Mama would not receive any more customers at that late hour, and the twenty or so who remained would soon be leaving. But shortly thereafter, it was not business as usual at Casa Del Mama.

At 9:15, a masked man armed with a nickel-plated revolver entered the restaurant and ordered Judy to give him the money in the cash register. While a hesitant Judy contemplated the consequences of refusing to comply with such an outrageous request, her mother-in-law emerged from the kitchen. Mama didn't take a masked man who wore sunglasses at night at all seriously. "Come on, cut out the games," she said, giving him a little nudge.

The robber immediately shoved her daughter-in-law against the wall and pointed his gun at Julia. "Lady, I mean business," he snarled. "If you don't hand over the money, I'll blow your head off!"

At that moment, a waitress heading toward the register saw what was happening and rushed into the kitchen screaming, "We're being robbed!"

While the startled cook called the police, the masked bandit grabbed the money and raced out the door, whereupon Sam took off in hot pursuit. But since a man in his late fifties couldn't outrun a man in his early twenties, Sam looked for his getaway car. However, the stick-up man was too smart to draw attention to himself by roaring off on screeching tires, as TV's fictional criminals invariably do in order to prevent viewers from switching to another channel.

Instead, the robber maintained a low profile and concentrated on

getting rid of all physical evidence connecting him with the crime —
including the money! He tore off his sunglasses, mask and shirt, and
discarded them along the Periwinkle bike path. After cutting
through the bank's parking lot, he crossed Casa Ybel Road and
buried his booty near an old alligator pond. Confident that he had
successfully dealt with all incriminating evidence, he climbed into
his car and drove off the island.

* * *

Alerted by the dispatcher who had received the call from Casa Del
Mama's cook, all members of the SPD, including auxiliaries, arrived
at the scene of the crime shortly after it was committed. In fact, the
robber was probably still digging around the alligator pond when
the police arrived at the restaurant. And for all I know, I might well
have passed the "perp" on my way over from Ft. Myers Beach.*

The SPD interviewed everyone present at the time of the robbery
and, in what the police call "doing a neighborhood," talked to everyone who might have been in the vicinity of Casa Del Mama around
that time. Much to the dismay of my young, inexperienced officers,
several hours of tedious work failed to produce a single lead. But
while I shared their discouragement, I wasn't at all surprised.

A quarter-century of police work had prepared me for the fact that
armed robberies are extremely difficult cases to solve, and for several reasons. With the exception of young girls in their late teens,
who take a keen interest in both men and clothes, few witnesses are
able to give the police a good description of the wanted subject.

Moreover, most armed bandits leave little or no evidence at the
scene of the crime. The police are lucky to obtain a description of the
getaway vehicle and the direction in which it was traveling. Unfortunately, the SPD had no such luck.

Witnesses, none of whom were teen-age girls, described the
masked bandit as a tall, slender, white male dressed in old clothes
and carrying a nickel-plated gun. Since he wore sunglasses under
the mask, his eyes were not visible. Moreover, the robber left no

---

* Since the SPD then comprised no more than a handful of officers and auxiliaries,
all became involved in the case.

physical evidence at the restaurant. And, worst of all, nobody saw his getaway vehicle. As a result, the SPD dispatcher who received the cook's call could not ask the county to raise the drawbridge on the causeway.*

Therefore, our dispatcher immediately called the Lee County Sheriff's Department and requested a roadblock for all traffic leaving the island. Thank God the deputy assigned to the boring roadblock that Monday night took his job seriously and duly recorded *everyone* who left the island. But our first real break in the case came later that evening, when a man walking on the Periwinkle bike path with his daughter found the robber's mask, sunglasses and shirt and turned them over to us.

Unfortunately, we could not immediately follow up on that lead. Sanibel had already closed down for the night, and few places of business would be open before 10:00 the next morning. But since the clock didn't stop ticking, every hour that passed reduced our chances of apprehending the robber. We were losing precious time, and there wasn't a damn thing I could do about it until Tuesday.

*   *   *

Tuesday morning, I directed Officers Ray Rhodes and Lew Phillips to take the shirt and sunglasses to every place of business on Periwinkle and ask if anyone could identify them. Although nobody did, Ray later received a call from one of Casa Del Mama's waitresses.

The latter reported that after Ray and Lew had left the restaurant, another waitress told her that the shirt and sunglasses belonged to her husband, Bret Williams. We brought a cooperative Mrs. Williams to SPD headquarters, where she identified the shirt and sunglasses and signed a statement to the effect that they belonged to Bret Taylor Williams, formerly a cook at Casa Del Mama.

* The County's bridge authority will raise the drawbridge whenever the SPD can provide some description of a suspect's vehicle. Indeed, it has done so many times. Since mainland crooks know this, the causeway's three-dollar toll and the bascule bridge serve to discourage them from committing crimes on Sanibel.

Case closed? Not by a long shot. I knew only too well that a pair of sunglasses and an old, long-sleeved shirt identified as belonging to Bret Williams did not constitute proof that he was the person wearing them when the crime was committed. In fact, Williams could easily refute such flimsy evidence by claiming that someone had stolen his shirt and sunglasses, or he had given them to Goodwill, or his wife was just trying to get back at him for fooling around with another woman. In order to nail the crooked cook, the SPD had to come up with more convincing evidence.

Later that day, a resident who lived just off Casa Ybel Road reported that the ground near the pond on his property had been disturbed. Since investigating this report involved digging, literally rather than figuratively, several SPD officers and auxiliaries rolled up their sleeves and proceeded to dig. They soon uncovered the loot the armed bandit had buried the night before — but not the gun.

*   *   *

Not surprisingly, the unearthed evidence didn't prove any connection between Bret Williams and the robbery. But thanks to the diligent deputy at the roadblock, the SPD could prove that Williams had been on the island when the crime was committed. The deputy's record, coupled with the wife's sworn statement, constituted reasonable grounds for searching Williams' apartment in Fort Myers. Unfortunately, the sun was now in the process of performing its daily disappearing act, and I knew that we couldn't wait until Wednesday morning to obtain a search warrant.

In police work, time is of the essence. In a free society, however, securing a search warrant is a very time-consuming proposition. "Hey, Della, run down to the courthouse and pick up a search warrant!" is the kind of fictional scene that occurs only on TV and in the movies. But since the SPD had to deal with hard facts rather than convenient fictions, Officers Rhodes, Phillips, and I drove to Fort Myers Tuesday evening. None of us came home that night.

In the eyes of the law, everyone is presumed innocent until proven guilty. Moreover, our Bill of Rights guarantees citizens freedom from unreasonable searches and seizures, or the use of general warrants.

Thus, like all American police departments, the SPD cannot secure a warrant to search the private premises of a presumably innocent person without first drawing up an affidavit that includes a description of the location and exterior of said premises, and very persuasive reasons for searching them. Subsequently, a judge must sign the search warrant.

In my opinion, such stringent requirements are both reasonable and essential. Without them, the United States would not be a free country in which the rights of all citizens, including criminal suspects, are fully protected. Therefore, after crossing the causeway on Tuesday evening, my men and I worked for hours in order to prepare an affidavit that ensured the full protection of Bret Taylor Williams' civil rights.

Since the affidavit required a description of the residence the SPD wanted to search, my first priority was to locate Williams' apartment in what was then the boondocks of East Fort Myers. We stopped to ask for directions, which left a lot to be desired, but finally succeeded in finding the apartment in question. Subsequently, we went to the Lee County Sheriff's Department in Fort Myers and met with Assistant State Attorney, Jim Thompson.

Although Jim jokingly advised us to "baffle them with bullshit," he spent several hours helping us draw up a strong affidavit that would not later be thrown out of court (along with any evidence found in the serach). If policemen were good typists, we might have completed the lengthy document by midnight. But since many of us rely on the hunt-and-peck method, it took somewhat longer. Thus, I had the dubious distinction of waking up a Lee County judge around 1:00 Wednesday morning.

The judge agreed to let us bring the affidavit to his home, where we spent some time discussing it. I quickly realized that the one-armed judge, who used to fly one of Lee County's large, mosquito-spraying aircraft, was not a man to be baffled by bullshit. Thanks to Jim Thompson, he didn't find any in our affidavit.

After the judge signed the search warrant, I contacted the Sheriff's Department and asked for a few deputies to meet us at Williams' apartment building. By 3:00 A.M., the deputies had the place surrounded and the SPD was ready to move in.

* * *

Of course, moving in did not involve bashing down the door and blazing away. A search warrant is not a license to conduct a SWAT-team operation. Instead, the police must knock on the door and announce their presence - even if they have good reason to believe that the person on the other side of the door is armed and considered dangerous.

Since I'd been trained to lead and take the most exposed position when I was in charge of an operation, I knocked on Williams' door. "This is the police! Open up!" I shouted, and quickly stepped aside in case Williams responded by firing at the door (in which event a 230-pound target over six-feet tall would certainly suffer the consequences).

Fortunately, Bret Williams was asleep, alone, and unarmed. When the drowsy suspect finally opened his door, I told him that we had a search warrant and read it to him. I also informed Williams that he was now under arrest, and read him his Miranda rights.

A bane in the eyes of law-enforcement officers, the Miranda rights are a blessing in the eyes of those who break the law. Even if the police actually see a killer shoot someone, they must read him his rights!

The politely phrased Miranda Warning advises people that they have the right to remain silent, for anything they say can and will be used against them in court. Moreover, should anyone seek to question them, arrested persons are entitled to legal representation and, if they can't afford a lawyer, the taxpayers will provide one. Finally, anyone placed under arrest is assured that he can decide to exercise his Miranda rights at any time, and refuse to answer any questions or make any statements.

Clearly, anyone who has committed a crime, and talks to the police is an idiot. But since twenty-three-year-old Bret Taylor Williams was not an idiot, he kept his mouth shut. I handcuffed him and had him sit in a chair so he could watch while we searched his apartment. Although we found a homemade mask similar to the one used in the armed robbery, a T-shirt with eyeholes cut out, it didn't have the telltale blue thread the robber had used to tie on his mask. But just as we were about to leave, Ray opened a cupboard and pulled out a spool of blue thread. Bingo!

* * *

After delivering Williams to the Lee County Jail, which in honor of Sheriff Frank Wanicka we called "Friendly Frank's Hotel," we celebrated the successful conclusion of our investigation over breakfast at a Fort Myers restaurant. I was particularly pleased by the fine cooperation we had received from all county law-enforcement agencies for, in my experience, such was not always the case. But above all, I was proud of the SPD. My small force of inexperienced officers and volunteer auxiliaries had performed extremely well, and put in 350 hours of overtime without a single complaint.

A former firefighter who had lived on Sanibel since he was a toddler, a claim few islanders can make, Ray Rhodes had worked on the case for twenty-six hours. He developed the first information that led to Williams' arrest on February 11, and also discovered the most important piece of evidence: the spool of blue thread. But since a policeman's pay bears no relation to his performance, it's essential to give outstanding officers some form of public recognition. Therefore, I nominated Ray for the Fort Myers *News-Press* quarterly Officer of the Year Award, and was delighted when he won it.

In the meantime, Bret Williams was scheduled to go to trial in July, and I felt that we had a solid case. For in addition to the testimony of Williams' wife and the deputy at the roadblock, the FBI had analyzed the blue thread and matched it right down to the cut with the thread found on the robber's mask. And since billboards throughout Florida in those days warned people that they would get three years to life for a crime committed with a gun, I was confident that Williams would spend a number of years behind bars. But such confidence caused me to forget an old adage: if you're guilty, go before a jury.

However, Williams' lawyer did not forget that adage. Well aware that juries are highly unpredictable and susceptible to visual impressions, the able defense attorney made sure that his client would look as innocent as a choirboy when he appeared in court. In fact, I hardly recognized Williams, who had his hair cut and wore a conservative suit, white shirt and a tie. In any event, the defendant and his attorney must have made a splendid impression on both the jury and the judge. The former found Bret Taylor Williams guilty of attempted grand larceny rather than armed robbery, and the latter sentenced him to serve one year in jail and pay a $1,000 fine.

In addition to being infuriated by the outcome of Williams' trial, I was totally frustrated by my inability to understand it. According to the prosecuting attorney, the jury had reduced the charge from armed robbery to attempted grand larceny for two reasons: the gun was never found, and Williams never got to keep any of the money he stole because the SPD discovered it! While I was grateful to the prosecutor for his explanation, it did nothing to lower my blood pressure. But, like most American law-enforcement officers, I resigned myself to the frustration inherent in protecting a society with a strong propensity for shooting itself in the foot.

But although Williams was lucky, his wife and two other waitresses employed by Casa Del Mama at the time of the robbery were not. All three died of unnatural causes. Williams' wife was found hanging from a tree in rural Immokalee. The waitress who had called Ray Rhodes was raped by a shrimper on Fort Myers Beach and he dumped her dead body into Matanzas Pass. And the third waitress, who later became the secretary for the Sanibel City Attorney, was found dead in a car at the bottom of a canal in Cape Coral—the Medical Examiner's report stated she had cocaine in her system.

The Islander   February 17, 1976   5

Casa Del Mama Robbed

LATE NEWS!!!

Sunday night, SPD Chief John Butler disclosed that the money stolen from the Island restaurant early last week had been recovered.

We understand a judicious and hard stint of special police "digging" (one way to say investigation) was responsible for the find. The SPD and its hard working officers & volunteers are to be commended for their fine work!

9:15 p.m. a tall, thin, masked man wearing sun glasses, old clothes, his palid white hands holding a nickle-plated revolver entered the Casa del Mama restaurant on Periwinkle, stepped up the cash register and told Sam's wife, Judy to hand over the money.

More than 20 people were in the restaurant having late dinner. A few near the door realized what was happening but were too frightened to move other than to put their precious belongings on the floor in hopes that the robber would not rip them off, too.

Judy did not want to open the register. The day's receipts were in that little box and she knew it....$1,627. Sam's mother came in, gave the robber a nudge and said "come on, cut out the games." The robber turned on her, pointed the gun at her, gave Judy a push which sent her up against the wall and said "Lady, I mean business! Hand over the money or I'll fire."

About the same moment a waitress coming toward the register saw what was happening, turned about face and ran into the kitchen, screamed at the cook, "We're being robbed.." The cook called the police. Within five minutes the police were on the scene, but the robber had, by then, taken the money and fled on foot.

Sam's father took off after him in hot persuit, followed him out to the road and watched him running away. There was no get-away car in sight.

The Lee County Sheriff's department brought bloodhounds which followed the scent but the trail soon ended in a pile of clothes that the robber had shed along the way.

Bret Taylor Williams, 23, of Fort Myers, was arrested at his home Wednesday morning by SPD Chief John Butler and SPD officers, John Metz and Ray Rhodes. He was taken to the County Jail, where he was released on $5,000 bond. Arraignment has been set for March 1.

C16   March 5, 1976   ISLAND REPORTER

Island's first armed robbery signals 'trouble in paradise' Merchants tighten security

"Though merchants are unwilling to elaborate on their new security measures, some say they have installed alarms, new safes and additional locks. A few have purchased guns."

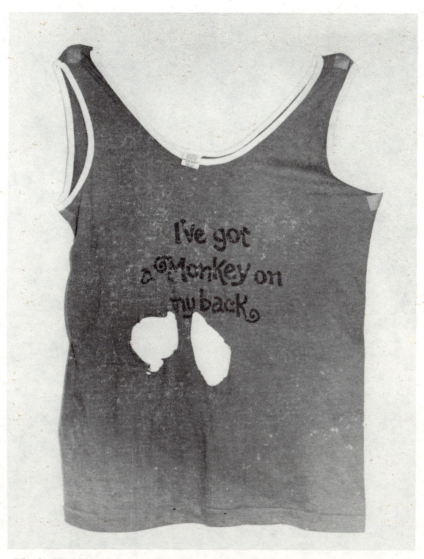

Mask used by stick-up man. Blue thread was used to tie on his mask.

BARE BUNS AT BOWMAN'S BEACH

One of Sanibel's most beautiful beaches is the narrow spit of sand between Old Blind Pass and the Gulf of Mexico. Named after the family that owned it before Lee County acquired it, Bowman's Beach attracts shellers, sunbathers, beachcombers, picnickers and, if the pass is open and teeming with mullet, fishermen. But in the mid-1970s, Bowman's Beach also attracted nudists.

In those days, Sanibel's last long stretch of undeveloped beach provided the kind of privacy and seclusion nudists seek. A good two miles away from the nearest paved road, Bowman's Beach was hard to find unless you knew which shell-paved "roads" and paths led to it. But the nudists who crossed the causeway knew how to get there, and so did the people who got a kick out of seeing them in the altogether. In fact, naturists, as they preferred to be called, were something of a tourist attraction.

Visitors who wanted to wow the folks back home in Ohio with stories about "nudies" made a beeline for Bowman's Beach, especially on weekends. While most came by car, some gawkers arrived by boat. If they failed to see any nudists baring their buns, they could always go shelling. And, who knows? They might find a junonia and get their pictures in the local papers!

* * *

23

Of course, I knew nothing about this special attraction when I became Chief of the SPD. Betty and I were still living on Fort Myers Beach, and Zee Butler had never mentioned nudism as a law-enforcement issue when she interviewed me. Since the nudists didn't parade all over the place or cause any trouble, she probably didn't consider them a problem. And, in fact, they were not a problem in the winter of '75.

But when the weather warmed up, the nudists returned to their favorite beach and, to borrow a popular phrase from those bygone days, let it all hang out. Appalled by public nudity, Paulette Burton launched an anti-nudist campaign during the merry month of May. The first of many peaceful protests that occurred during my years as Chief of Police, Paulette's was extremely effective. It also taught me a great deal about islanders.

Although few in number, Sanibelians undoubtedly surpass national averages in terms of involvement in community affairs. But while local issues often transform them into "concerned" citizens determined to "save" Sanibel from one evil or another, islanders never take to the streets. Instead, they gain publicity by writing letters to the editor, and exert political pressure by appearing before the city council - frequently armed with petitions.

Paulette Burton appeared before council with a petition signed by some fifty residents demanding an end to nudism on Sanibel. Speaking in a soft voice with a pronounced New England accent, Paulette expressed her outrage as a mother, grandmother, registered voter and taxpayer. Few politicians are willing to defy such an apple-pie combination, and members of Sanibel's first council were no exception.

Council readily agreed that state laws prohibiting indecent exposure certainly applied to Sanibel. The *Islander Reporter* quoted Mayor Goss as saying "nudity is now out of hand," and I received formal instructions to put an end to nudity at Bowman's Beach. Off the record, however, one disgruntled council member told me that the next step would be a law against skinny-dipping in your own swimming pool! Translation: "John, don't be too tough on the nudies."

Since it's not at all uncommon for politicians to say one thing publicly and another privately, a police chief's survival often depends on his ability to walk through a minefield without setting off an explosion. So before taking any action at Bowman's Beach, I read State Statute 800.03 very carefully. While I didn't expect "Exposure of sexual organs" to tell me how to deal with people who publicly exposed said organs, I hoped the statute would define what constituted *illegal* exposure. It didn't.

S.S. 800.03 is a politician's daydream and a policeman's nightmare: "It shall be unlawful for any person to expose or exhibit his sexual organs in any public place…in a vulgar or indecent manner …" But "vulgar" and "indecent" are not defined. Like beauty, they lie in the eyes of the beholder.

* * *

While thinking about beholders, I remembered the man who appeared before the Liquor Commission in Columbus, Ohio, on behalf of a girl charged with dancing in a "lewd, lascivious and obscene manner." The eyewitness testified that he and his wife had occupied front-row seats at the liquor establishment in question, and neither of them had considered the defendant's dancing the least bit lewd, lascivious or obscene.

After nearly an hour of such testimony, the weary judge dismissed this man with the traditional, "You may step down." But as the latter proceeded to do so, the judge suddenly felt inspired to pose a simple question: "What is obscene to you?" Following a few moments of reflection, the witness looked the judge straight in the eye and replied, "Nothing."

However, unlike the witness who blew his entire testimony with one word, the naturists at Bowman's Beach could reasonably argue that they were not exposing their sexual organs in a vulgar or indecent manner. Seeking privacy rather than public exposure, they generally flocked to the far end of the beach.

Moveover, not all were stark naked. Some women just stripped to the waist. But since breasts are not sexual organs, I couldn't arrest bare-breasted women for violating S.S. 800.03. Therefore, I decided that the best way to get rid of the nudists (without being too tough on them), was to enforce the laws against driving on the beach and trespassing on private property.*

Accompanied by the *Island Reporter's* Mark Twombly, I drove the SPD's new 4-wheel drive to Bowman's Beach on Memorial Day, 1975. While young, long-haired Mark was busy interviewing nudies (and removing all his clothes for the benefit of those who refused to talk to him until he did), I informed several dozen people that it was illegal to drive their cars on the beach, and warned them that the SPD would henceforth enforce that law.

I also told nearly a dozen nudists that the SPD would enforce S.S. 800.03 (without taking off my clothes in order to convey that information). But in some cases, communication placed me in an extremely delicate situation. Since I'm over six feet tall, it's absolutely impossible for me to look most women in the eyes without looking down. But if I looked too far down at the bare-breasted women at Bowman's Beach, some of whom were magnificently endowed, they might accuse *me* of approaching *them* in a vulgar or indecent manner! Fortunately, none did.

As a result of my friendly little visit on Memorial Day, word got around that the party was over: no more driving on the beach, no more trespassing on private property, and no more nudism. The SPD kept a close eye on Bowman's Beach for several weeks, citizens no longer complained about "goings-on" up there, and I thought we had the problem licked. Unfortunately, the nudists came back to Bowman's Beach the following year.

* * *

Publicity was primarily responsible for the rebirth of nudism in 1976. Articles in naturist publications featured Bowman's Beach as the perfect playground, an isolated paradise where "several hundred romp around burning their buns."

Then, in October, "Nudity Tolerated at Bowman's" appeared on the front page of the Fort Myers High School newspaper! The young

---

* The most popular illegal beach access was the property owned by the developers of Blind Pass Condominiums. Since construction was about to begin, the developers planned to put up a fence and hire a security guard to prevent trespassing.

author of that particular article assured his readers that people of all ages who enjoyed "letting it all hang out, literally" could do so at Bowman's without being bothered by the SPD.

Thanks to such publicity, Alice Kyllo, a landscape painter who often spent the entire day at the beach, saw scores of naked people she wouldn't dream of immortalizing on canvas. She considered some highly distasteful, and others downright disgusting. The former included fat women with breasts drooping down to their waists ("they should have worn a muumuu"), pot-bellied men ("they sure had nothing to be proud of" either above or below the waist), and "herds" of human animals whose exhibitionism was clearly "a form of mental illness."

But what really got Alice all riled up was public copulation, masturbation, and teenage Peeping Toms hiding in the bushes. Outraged by the realization that families with children and grandchildren would doubtless be exposed to such sights, she decided to take matters into her own hands. A staunch supporter of Paulette Burton's anti-nudist campaign in May of '75, Alice Kyllo launched another crusade in November '76 by writing a letter to the editor of the Fort Myers *News Press*.*

Alice's letter informed nudists that the following Sunday at 3:30 P.M., she would appear at Bowman's Beach armed with a shotgun and commence firing. Alice received calls from over a dozen people who wanted to enlist in her blast-their-buns brigade, and "Uncle" Clarence provided several guns loaded with rock salt.* Fortunately, a concerned reporter from the *Islander* told me about all this on the eve of the scheduled showdown. *Holy Jesus!*

I immediately sent one of my best officers, Ray Rhodes, over to Alice's house. He explained that people who took exception to her letter might well bring *their* guns to Bowman's Beach the following day and return fire, with the result that somebody was bound to be hurt and not necessarily in the behind.

* Since Alice had good reason to believe that members of the Sanibel Naturists group and other nudists who flocked to Bowman's Beach were not island residents, she sent her letter to the major newspaper distributed throughout Lee County.

* "Uncle" Clarence Rutland, a former lighthouse keeper and long-time resident, was then in his eighties.

A law-abiding citizen, Alice Kyllo was not about to break one law in order to enforce another. Moreover, she certainly didn't want her anti-nudist crusade to cause severe injury to anyone, including nudies. Therefore, Alice gave Ray her shotgun, lovingly loaded by Uncle Clarence, and readily agreed to support the SPD's peaceful approach to the nudist problem.

Accompanied by two plainclothes police officers, Alice walked the beach Sunday afternoon. Upon her complaint, the officers arrested two men for indecent exposure, one of whom had to swim back out to his boat to retrieve his wallet. When other nudists realized what was going on, they either put on their clothes or ran away. Naturally, the press got a big kick out of Operation Bare Buns.

Local newspapers featured humorous headlines like "Nudists Spared Salting" and "Plainclothesmen Arrest Noclothesmen On Bowman's." While it took the Miami *Herald* nearly eighteen months to latch on to the story, they compensated for the delay by coming up with the largest and longest headline: "Sanibel Artist Wins Long Struggle To Oust Nudes Cluttering Her View."

But although Alice Kyllo had clearly won the first battle, she realized that it marked the beginning rather than the end of her anti-nudist crusade. In a letter commending the SPD for "the very efficient way they carried out the arrests for obscenity and nudity at Bowman's Beach," Alice discussed the nudist problem in her typically forthright manner:

> "This should be a very good beginning for cleaning up this beach so residents and their guests and grandchildren can freely walk this beautiful beach without fear of being exposed to this sort of thing. We do not want the reputation of our island smirched (sic) by these characters who are evidently very much in need of mental therapy."

A few days after Alice's letter appeared in the *Reporter*, somebody butchered her caged bird with a pair of pruning shears. Shortly thereafter, someone poisoned her angora kitten. And one day, when Alice and a friend were walking on Bowman's Beach, a group of nudists suddenly surrounded them, shouted obscenities and threatened, "We're going to get 'em! We'll fix 'em!" Fortunately, a group of picnickers appeared and the nudists beat a hasty retreat.

In addition to the above, Alice was deluged with dirty telephone calls, generally in the middle of the night. While most callers concentrated on obscenity, one actually threatened to kill her! Tired of having her sleep interrupted for several weeks, Alice finally contacted the SPD. But when she realized that putting a trap and trace on her phone would only serve to trace the origin of obscene calls rather than prevent them from occurring, Alice came up with a practical solution: she stopped answering her phone at ungodly hours.

Not surprisingly, nudism at Bowman's Beach didn't come to an abrupt end in 1976. Thanks to previous publicity to the contrary, many people were unaware of the fact that the SPD was now enforcing S.S. 800.03. But when Florida newspapers carried an AP (Associated Press) story about our arresting seven nude men in March, 1980, naturists soon realized that Bowman's Beach was no longer an island paradise where they could "romp around burning their buns." As a result, nudism is no longer a problem for either concerned Sanibel citizens or the Sanibel Police Department.

Yet, although the Sanibel Naturists have stopped coming to Bowman's Beach, they continue to lobby for a portion of some beach in Lee County where they can let it all hang out both literally and legally. Thus, in recent years, the naturist crusade has attracted the attention of local radio and TV stations.

But when the media invited Alice Kyllo to discuss nudism with naturists, the latter doubtless wished they had never agreed to a joint interview. And no wonder. Alice made them look ridiculous with remarks like, "If you have something to exhibit, you should donate it to the Smithsonian."

THERE IS GOING TO BE BLOODSHED!

In the eyes of the public, the worst calls police receive are reports of murders, robberies, rapes, and other dastardly deeds. But in the eyes of the police, "domestics" are the calls they dread the most. For since domestic situations are totally unpredictable, death is frequently a distinct possibility.

Many years ago, when my partner and I responded to a family-trouble call in Mansfield, Ohio, we found a man standing behind the living-room couch aiming an automatic rifle at us. "Take one more step and I'll put five of these in your belly!" shouted the father of the polite little boy who had let us in the house. Luckily, we were able to talk the distraught father into giving us his weapon - and tossed him in jail.

I didn't expect to be involved in such life-threatening situations when I became chief of police on a tiny barrier island, whose law-abiding citizens were primarily concerned about traffic control. But some eighteen months later, I was looking down the barrel of an automatic pistol - held by a drunk and deeply disturbed man.

* * *

On November 1, 1976, Donald Hiers turned forty. Unfortunately, no one was home to wish him a happy birthday. His wife had recently moved out, and his young son had moved in with a family friend. Not surprisingly, Hiers hit the bottle and, by mid-afternoon, all became clear.

Since Helga had left no forwarding address, Hiers didn't know the whereabouts of his wife, whom he desperately wanted back. However, he did know the address of Gay Elder, the friend who was providing a safe haven for his sixteen-year-old son, John, whom he also wanted back. Therefore, Hiers grabbed his pistol and headed for Donax Street in his pickup truck.

When he arrived at Gay Elder's home, Hiers got into a violent argument with the woman who tried to protect his son. He abruptly ended the argument by firing his gun, and subsequently forced the terrified teenager to leave with him.

Fortunately, I was at the station at 4:57 P.M. when Gay called about a man shooting a gun on Donax Street. "Step on the button, and don't let her hang up!" I shouted to the dispatcher as I ran out the door.

Normally, a police chief doesn't have to remind the dispatcher what to do in an emergency. For any well-trained dispatcher knows how critical it is to keep the primary source of information on the phone, and immediately pushes the button that transmits the complainant's call to the patrol cars. But since the SPD dispatcher on duty was totally inexperienced, I could only hope that she would keep her head and follow my instructions.

Fortunately, she remembered to step on the foot button, and the call was patched to the SPD's only cruiser. Officer Don Case immediately drove to Gay Elder's home, and I heard his report to the dispatcher on my car radio. The name of the gunman in question was Donald Hiers. He had abducted his son and left the area in his pickup, license number and direction of travel unknown.

While I'd never met Hiers, a contractor and long-time resident, I knew who he was. For less than a week ago, Hiers had tried to kill himself by taking an overdose of drugs. Don Case arrested him under the provisions of the Baker Act, and we thought Hiers was still in the psychiatric ward of Lee Memorial Hospital.

Although we now knew he was out, we didn't know where he was. Nor did we know that the demented man had just told his captive son, "There is going to be bloodshed - either me or Helga or someone else - but there's going to be bloodshed."

While Hiers was scaring the hell out of young John, my car radio crackled and Don came back on the air. "This is one-oh-six. Hiers is at his house on Lindgren - he's holding the kid hostage. That's 947 Lindgren Boulevard."

"One-oh-six, this is one-oh-one," I replied. "I'm at MacIntosh. Hold the fort until I get there." The reference to my precise location, Sanibel's book store, was standard operating procedure (SOP). For an officer waiting for backup needs to know when help is likely to arrive.

A few minutes later, I arrived at the Spanish-style home in time to see Don Case take off his gun belt and walk in the door. Hiers was holding a gun on him.

Holy Christ!

* * *

Recently released from the loony bin, the man who now held *two* hostages was obviously violent, and quite possibly drunk. Fortunately, I had some training in hostage situations.

I should immediately order my men to cover all four corners of the house, and assign an officer to come up with a layout of its interior. I should also direct an officer to call Hiers from a neighbor's home to determine the nature of his problem and the requirements for resolving it - without killing his hostages in the process. Finally, I should station a few snipers in strategic locations so they could shoot Hiers if he refused to be reasonable.

However, standard operating procedure presumes that the police are equipped with such things as bullet-proof vests, bull horns, tear gas, and gas masks. But the SPD had none of the preceding. SOP also presumes the availability of manpower, preferably experienced. But at the time, the SPD boasted a grand total of six officers - and I was the only one with any experience.

Thus, as soon as I saw Don Case drop his gun belt and enter Hiers' house, I contacted the dispatcher. "This is one-oh-one. Call the sheriff and tell him we've got one helluva hostage situation over here and I need all the help he can give us. And ask him to bring over some tear gas. We might have to gas this son of a bitch."

After issuing those instructions, I turned my attention to observing and pondering the situation while waiting for the Lee County Sheriff's Department to show up. But I derived no comfort from what I saw. The ground-level home was protected by the canal behind it. Moreover, numerous windows provided views from every direction, unobstructed by vegetation.

My thoughts were no more comforting than my observations. For the forty-seven-year-old grandfather inside the house was my least experienced officer. A former commercial fisherman and restaurateur, Don Case was fresh out of recruit school. If Hiers decided to shoot Case or the kid...

My depressing thoughts were interrupted by the arrival of Don Whitehead, editor of the *Island Reporter* and Hiers' next-door neighbor. "What's going on, Chief?"

I quickly filled him in and braced myself for a steady stream of suggestions. But the ex-CIA agent offered no advice. For at that moment, a Lee County Sheriff's deputy pulled in. I immediately brought the deputy up to date, and reiterated our requests for equipment and manpower.

Unlike many law-enforcement agencies, the SPD and the Lee County Sheriff's department operated in the spirit of cooperation rather than rivalry. But while I was confident the LCSD would help us out, I remained deeply concerned about what might happen before they crossed the causeway. For at any moment, Hiers might decide to kill either one or both of his hostages.

"Hey, do you have a vest?" I asked the sheriff's deputy. "Yup, I'm wearin' it," he drawled, pointing his thumb toward the shirt that covered his bullet-proof vest.

"Mind if I borrow it for a while?"

"Be my guest," said the deputy, who promptly stripped to the waist and gave me his life-saving vest.

Wearing the protective vest under a polo shirt and a jacket, I walked to the front of the house, opened the door, and slipped inside. Glancing into the living room, I quickly sized up the situation. The three were seated in a triangular formation with Hiers at the apex, a geometric arrangement that enabled him to keep an eye on son John while pointing his pistol at Don. I stepped out of the foyer and entered the room.

"Don't take another step!" Hiers shouted. "I've seen you cops on TV and I know all your tricks!"

"Hey, I'm not trying to trick you - I'm here to help you. Look, I'm unarmed," I said, pulling back my jacket and slowly turning around so he could see that I wasn't carrying any concealed weapons. Fortunately, Hiers was so impressed by my pirouette that he didn't ask me to roll up my pants - a request that would have revealed the Colt .38 in a holster strapped to the inside of my left leg.

"Okay...but you've gotta sit over there," he growled, pointing his pistol toward the far end of the couch. "And don't try to get any closer to me."

Thus, the Chief of the SPD became hostage No. 3.

* * *

By this time, the sheriff had plenty of men in place. And since the media had picked up the police radio traffic, TV crews were also stationed outside the house. Such exciting activity caused passersby to gather around, and even Morgan House, Chief of the Fort Myers P.D., came over to see what he could do to help us. But there was nothing anyone outside could do until we made a move *inside* the house.

In hostage situations, it's essential to do two things: keep the guy with the gun talking, and promise to move heaven and earth to get him what he wants. Thus, while Don and I looked down the barrel of his cocked, automatic pistol, we talked with Hiers and learned that he wanted Helga.

Of course, there was no way I would allow Helga (or anyone else), to enter the home and become yet another hostage. My top priority was to get the boy safely out of the house, and take it from there. Fortunately, my new recruit not only reached the same conclusion, but also found a way to free John without risking anyone's life.

Unlike me, Don Case knew Hiers well. Both men had lived on the island a number of years, and they played on the same softball team.

And although Case had arrested Hiers less than a week ago, the latter didn't appear to hold that against him. Thus, Don succeeded in convincing Hiers that his best chance of being reunited with his wife lay in releasing his son. For once John was free, he would try to find Helga and bring her home.

When John finally walked out of the house, the crowd cheered - and the reporters rushed over to get a statement. Given his harrowing experience, the boy was remarkably coherent. John explained that his father was deeply depressed by Helga's disappearance and had been drinking heavily. "He gets really belligerent and mean and his whole expression changes and he looks vicious and crazy. He's mentally disturbed and needs help and I'm afraid of him, and I know that he would do physical harm."

Of course, Don and I didn't hear John's statement. But we didn't need to hear it, for we knew only too well that the man holding a gun on us was drunk, demented, and dangerous. We also knew that, without Helga, our chances for survival were nil.

Therefore, we kept on talking to Hiers, constantly assuring him that we were going to do everything possible to find his wife. Fortunately, the friendly, conversational approach produced positive results: Hiers calmed down, and became receptive to seemingly helpful suggestions.

"Hey, you want a beer or something?" I asked.

"Yeah, get me a beer. There's some in the kitchen. But don't try anything funny!" he warned, pointing his pistol at Don's head. The meaning was all too clear.

I assured Hiers I wouldn't pull any tricks, and brought him a can of beer. Luckily, the gunman didn't realize that the drink served a dual purpose: it put him at ease, and occupied one of his hands.

At that point, Don and I would have welcomed such liquid refreshment. For while fear had caused our adrenalin to flow, it had also made our mouths so dry we could hardly speak. But since survival was contingent upon talking our way out of this perilous confrontation, we kept up a steady stream of conversation.

While this was certainly not the first time my life had been on the line, it was the first time anyone had held a gun on me for well over an hour. However, I'd been trained to deal with such situations in the following manner: (1) gain the gunman's confidence by promising to get whatever he wants; (2) discuss the difficulties involved in meeting his demands; (3) volunteer to help him overcome those obstacles. I could only hope that such a winning combination would work with a man who was totally out of control.

While Hiers was comfortably ensconced in a chair and sipping his beer, I brought up a problem that had "suddenly" occurred to me. "You know," I began, "there's just one thing that bothers me." Hiers was now all ears. "I mean, your boy's out there looking for his mother, but he's all alone - nobody's helping him!"

Having outlined the problem, I immediately offered to provide the solution. Specifically, I told Hiers I would alert every law-enforcement agency in the Fort Myers area to Helga's disappearance, and ask them to help us find her. "So, if you'll just let me talk to one of the deputies outside, I'll tell him to get right on it and —"

"No! You can't go outside!" Hiers shrieked, spilling beer on his shirt and clenching his gun.

The beer-stained shirt didn't bother me, but the cocked automatic did. For the man with his finger on the trigger was now extremely agitated, and clearly on the verge of spinning out of control. If I failed to defuse the situation, Don and I wouldn't have much of a future.

"Look," I said soothingly. "I'm not talking about going outside. All I'm saying is the police will immediately start looking for Helga the minute I tell them she's disappeared."

The idea of an immediate and massive manhunt for his wayward wife calmed Hiers considerably. "So," I continued, "all I have to do to get this thing going is open the front door and pass the word. I'll stand right by the door so you can watch me the whole time."

Since his desire to find Helga was greater than his distrust, Hiers agreed to let me open the door and talk to one of the deputies. "Tell everyone out there not to do *anything*," I muttered. "I think we can get this guy."

Following my brief conversation with the sheriff's deputy, I closed the door and returned to the living room. "Well?" said Hiers.

"Everything's all set," I assured him. "They're gonna put out an APB (all-points bulletin, TV talk for Hiers' benefit). It shouldn't take them too long to find Helga."

Of course, it also wouldn't take Hiers too long to suspect that I was lying. And before he did, I had to figure out some way to "get this guy."

*   *   *

A hostage stands no chance against a gunman who is suspicious and impatient, in addition to being drunk and deranged. Thus, the key to our survival lay in convincing Hiers that we were constantly thinking of ways to get him what he wanted sooner rather than later. In this connection, another thought "suddenly" occurred to me.

"Holy shit! I forgot about the airport!"

"Whaddya mean the airport?"

"I mean, your wife could be down at Page Field waiting to get on a plane!"

Momentarily stunned by this revelation, Hiers quickly recovered. "Can't you stop her?" he asked, now sounding rather plaintive.

"Sure, we can stop her," I said. "But first, I've got to call the dispatcher and tell her what to do. Okay if I use the phone?"

"Yeah, go ahead. There's one in the kitchen. But don't try any of your cop tricks!" he warned. "I'll be watching you and listening to every word you say."

I stepped over to the kitchen, reached for the wall phone, and dialed the SPD dispatcher. "Call the airport right away and tell them to hold all outgoing flights. And send some police down there to help them look for Helga Hiers. You got that?"

I hoped the inexperienced dispatcher wouldn't believe me, and prayed that Donald Hiers would. Fortunately, he did - and never knew how close I came to killing him.

While talking to the dispatcher, I could see Hiers just as clearly as he could see me. All I had to do was drop the phone "accidentally," a perfect excuse for bending over. Then, instead of picking up the phone, I'd pull out my Colt .38 and blow his head off. At such close range, I couldn't miss.

But since Hiers had his trigger on an automatic aimed at Don

Case, I knew I couldn't shoot him. For if I did, his gun would probably go off. Unwilling to run such a risk, I returned to my designated seat, pondered the situation, and concluded that our only hope lay in disarming the gunman.

"You know," I mused, "they might've had some luck down there at the airport. You want me to call the dispatcher back and find out for you?" Hiers couldn't resist such an offer, and readily agreed.

Following a few words with the dispatcher, I lured Hiers into the kitchen by shouting, "She says they've found Helga!" But while highly excited by my announcement, Hiers didn't forget to bring Don with him.

"Here, you talk to her," I said, handing him the receiver.

With Hiers now holding a phone in one hand and a gun in the other, I knew this was the time to disarm him. I'd never disarmed anyone holding a gun on me - but I suddenly remembered everything Konan had taught me.

* * *

Small, lean, mean, and a black belt, Konan Yudanshakai was a judo instructor at the Mansfield, Ohio YMCA. Shortly before retiring from the MPD, I asked my men to sign up for Konan's six-week course. And since I never asked anyone to do anything I wouldn't do, I signed up, too.

It soon became apparent that many of us were, to put it charitably, somewhat out of shape. For while throwing each other around, we succeeded in fracturing clavicles and dislocating hips. Fortunately, however, the primary emphasis was on disarming techniques. As a result, and despite the fact that I was now a fifty-year-old grandfather and no longer a white belt, Konan's training saved our lives.

I grabbed Hiers' gun with both hands and drew it away from my body (for the pistol would probably go off and the family jewels - or other vital organs - would suffer the consequences). After a short struggle, the gun hit the floor, and I hit Hiers as hard as I could. I saw his eyes roll in their sockets, but he didn't go down. So, I slugged him again, and he finally sank to the kitchen floor.

We immediately slapped a pair of handcuffs on Hiers, keeping his hands safely behind his back. Don picked up the automatic (which, by some miracle, never went off), and we marched our prisoner out the front door. Not surprisingly, we were immediately surrounded by a phalanx of photographers, and temporarily blinded by their flashbulbs.

When Don and I finished giving statements to the press, I walked around and thanked the deputies for their fine help and support. Indeed, the LCSD did an outstanding job of keeping things under control, realizing that any commotion outside the house would endanger the lives of the hostages inside.

At one point during our two-hour ordeal, Hiers became so angry when a helicopter hovered overhead that I was sure he would shoot us. Luckily, the LCSD quickly got rid of the chopper, while Don and I continued to talk about Helga.

But what I didn't know was that a deputy "dog man" had been standing outside the kitchen window, waiting for us to move out of the way so he could get a clear shot at Hiers. For the deputy's dog never made a sound. Thus, thanks to Konan's training, the LCSD's control, and a silent dog, I was still alive. I was also sweating bullets, and my mouth was bone dry.

In the never-never world of TV, a policeman who has just survived a life-threatening situation will soon be off French-kissing some girl. But in the real world, there's a time for fear and a time for love - and the two don't coincide. When I returned home that night, I could barely summon enough energy to give Betty a chaste peck on the cheek.

*   *   *

Charged once again under the Baker Act, Donald Hiers spent a few nights in the Lee County Jail. He was then transferred from Friendly Frank's Hotel to a state mental hospital in Arcadia, where he remained for some ninety days. Upon his release and return to Sanibel, we arrested Hiers and charged him with four counts of aggravated assault. However, he never went to court.

In police work, one of the frustrating facts of life is that it's almost impossible to obtain a conviction against anyone who has graduated from a "funny farm." Indeed, prosecutors are not at all interested in pressing charges in such no-win cases that reduce their success rates and diminish their reputations. But a policeman can't pick and choose his cases; he has to cope with every misguided individual who comes down the pike.

As a result, some officers become so frustrated by the revolving door of the "crimimal injustice system" that they decide not to bust their butts or lay their lives on the line. Instead, they sit safely inside their cruisers, are slow to respond to dangerous situations, and generally arrive on the scene when the action is over. They never chase a bad guy, let alone catch one. But they issue lots of speeding and parking tickets. For whether they do their job well or poorly, they receive the same salary on payday.

In my experience, the best way to prevent the frustrations inherent in law enforcement from turning a good policeman into a lousy public servant is to provide the kind of motivation money can't buy: public recognition. Thus, whenever I received a letter commending one of my officers, I gave a copy to the local press. And when an officer's performance was exceptional, I nominated him for the monthly Law Enforcement Outstanding Performance Award sponsored by the Fort Myers *News-Press*.

After I submitted Don's name, the editors reviewed the hostage incident and added my name to their list of nominees. Don and I subsequently received the November award: engraved walnut plaques, $25 savings bonds, and a great deal of public recognition. A few months later, at the annual *News-Press* banquet for some one hundred lawmen and guests, the state attorney general presented us with the coveted Southwest Florida Law Enforcement Officer of the Year Award: engraved walnut plaques, $100 savings bonds, and a thunderous round of applause.

Overcome with emotion, Don and I hugged each other, shook hands, and then embraced again. "This doesn't seem real," said a beaming Don Case. "I've been a cop for less than a year, but it's the greatest profession going. This award is just super!"

But while everything was going well for the SPD, nothing was going well for Donald Hiers.

* * *

Shortly before Don and I received the annual award, Hiers was released from the mental hospital in Arcadia and returned to his home on Lindgren. However, Helga refused to join him. Instead, she divorced her husband, who became abusive when he'd had too much to drink, and moved to California.

After losing his wife in the winter of '78, Hiers lost his son in the summer. John fell from the bow of a boat plying the waters off the nearby island of Cayo Costa, and was cut to pieces by the propeller. Somehow, Hiers managed to survive those losses. He remarried, and began a new life with Judy.

For the next few years, the Hiers couple appeared to be happy. Judy worked with her husband in his construction business, which soon began to thrive. She played softball on the women's team, he played softball on the men's team, and they played together on a bowling team. Thus, no one was prepared for the dreadful tragedy that occurred on March 21, 1982.

On that fateful Sunday afternoon, Hiers drove down Sanibel-Captiva Road to the American Legion and started drinking. The more he drank, the more he talked about his son's death - a catastrophe from which he had never recovered. Then, when he was quite drunk, Hiers told people at the bar that he had three, 5-gallon cans of gasoline and was going to blow up his house and his wife. Unfortunately, nobody believed him.

Thus, although Hiers left the club around dinner time, we didn't receive a call about his threats until 7:40 P.M. Officers Don Case and Betty Weir rushed to his home on Lindgren Boulevard, and arrived in time to hear a violent argument going on inside. But as the officers walked toward the door, two explosions brought an abrupt end to the altercation, and the house suddenly burst into flames.

Hearing ungodly screams, Don ran to the back of the house and found Judy Hiers fleeing from the screened porch, her body engulfed in flames. He put out the fire and dragged her to the front of the house, where Betty Weir administered artificial respiration.

Severely burned from the waist down, Judy was immediately transported to Lee Memorial Hospital, and subsequently transferred to a burn center in Texas. After months of excruciating pain,

Judy Hiers finally recovered and returned to Sanibel. Alas, there was nothing the SPD could do for Donald Hiers.

Since Hiers' body was puffed up like a basketball and burned beyond recognition, positive identification was based primarily on his belt buckle and dentures. The Medical Examiner listed burning from flash combustion as the cause of death, and islanders drew a little comfort from the knowledge that the man who had been tormented for so many years died instantly.

DONALD HIERS LED FROM HIS SANIBEL HOME AFTER HOLDING LAWMEN AT GUNPOINT...lawmen said the contractor was despondent over family problems.

**JOHN HIERS
...father released him.**

SANIBEL POLICE CHIEF JOHN BUTLER AND PATROLMAN DON CASE...News-Press recognized pair for bravery in island incident.

MARY JANE

The wild hemp plant grows in nearly every part of the world, and man has made use of it since time immemorial. Indeed, the strong fiber of its stalk has been transformed into a host of useful items ranging from coarse ropes to fine fabrics. Unwilling to waste any part of the plant, people ate and smoked its flowers and leaves, and were delighted by the feeling of euphoria they induced.

Scientists called the plant *Cannabis*, a fancy word for hemp which they borrowed from the ancient Greeks, who borrowed it from the even more ancient Scythians, who undoubtedly borrowed it from somebody else. But while scientists had only one name for the plant, those who smoked it had many. Egyptians called it hashish, Indians called it bhang, and Americans called it marijuana - otherwise known as Mary Jane.

In 1948, the year I joined the MPD (Mansfield Police Department in Ohio), marijuana was not a problem in that industrial town. In fact, it wasn't a problem in any American city. For Mary Jane's clientele was largely limited to prostitutes, Mexican railroad workers, musicians seeking inspiration, and bums seeking blissful oblivion. People were not afraid to go anywhere at night, the police walked their beats, and young people regarded law-enforcement officers as friends and protectors.

In the 1950s, life with Mary Jane remained essentially the same. Thus, when the MPD arrested a "low-life" for possession of a Prince Albert tobacco can filled with marijuana, he received a speedy trial and spent time in the state penitentiary. For Americans still believed illegal drugs were dreadful, and those who used them belonged in jail. The courts didn't nitpick over the amount of marijuana involved (or how the police happened to find it), and society supported the law-enforcement efforts of "Our Friend, The Policeman." Unfortunately, the following decade marked the beginning of the reign of Mary Jane.

*   *   *

During the swinging sixties, a number of movie stars, rock stars, and other high-profile personalities suddenly stopped hiding their use of drugs. In fact, many made a point of publicizing an addiction for which they made no apologies, and felt no shame. Thus, given the star quality now associated with drugs in general and marijuana in particular, Mary Jane entered the mainstream of American society - where it was often referred to as pot, grass, tea, and the weed.

Since the weed was cheap, nobody had to rob a 7-Eleven to pay for it. Unfortunately, a host of other illegal drugs appeared on the scene: amphetamines and barbiturates, uppers and downers, cocaine, heroin, LSD, etc. They provided a much bigger kick than Mary Jane, and were also far more expensive and addictive. Thus the people who became hopelessly hooked on such powerful drugs often turned to crime in order to pay for a quick fix. As a result, armed robbery (once a rare crime), became one of the most common crimes committed in the United States.

Not surprisingly, the country changed considerably during the sixties. All kinds of violent crimes became so common that people were afraid to walk anywhere at night. Citizens took to the streets to protest one thing or another, and peaceful "civil disobedience" often ended in violence and tragedy. Young people rebelled against any form of authority, and frequently called policeman "pigs."

However, drugs were by no means to blame for everything that happened during the reign of Mary Jane. Indeed, a confluence of factors caused the social upheaval associated with the sixties. Chief among them were the civil rights movement, a series of assassinations (President Kennedy, his brother Bobby, Martin Luther King), and the Vietnam War. Never before had young American men shouted, "Hell, no! We won't go!" After all, the U.S. Attorney General and Jane Fonda publicly supported the enemy without ever being tried for treason.

In addition to serious domestic disturbances, a highly unpopular war, and mind-altering drugs, other factors contributed to the radical changes that took place in the sixties. Some people blamed the "boob tube" for promoting violence by showing so much of it on the TVs now installed in millions of American homes. Others blamed Dr. Benjamin Spock's best-selling book on baby care for encouraging parents to be permissive. In their eyes, the pediatrician's spineless advice had produced spoiled brats, an instant-gratification generation of potheads who flocked to Woodstock, NY - and destroyed a kind-hearted farmer's alfalfa field.

In any event, urban policemen suddenly had to deal with an astronomical increase in illegal drugs, violent crimes, and "peaceful demonstrations" that turned into riots. Fortunately, the federal government sent me (and countless other command officers) to the U.S. Army's Military Police School in Georgia, where we learned how to restore and maintain law and order. Unfortunately, the U.S. Supreme Court rendered several decisions that made it extremely difficult for us to do either of the preceding.

Foremost was the Miranda decision in 1966, which required us to recite a litany of rights to the people we planned to arrest. Yet despite the Miranda decision, hordes of white middle-class people continued to be arrested for using or possessing Mary Jane. Not surprisingly, politicians suddenly felt compelled to take another look at the laws concerning illegal drugs, and the courts felt a similar compulsion. As a result, many drug crimes were reduced from felonies to misdemeanors, previous methods of obtaining evidence were frequently ruled inadmissible in court, and in some parts of the country a small amount of Mary Jane no longer counted because it didn't weigh enough on the scales of justice.

Thus, when the newly incorporated City of Sanibel hired me to establish the SPD in 1975, I was greatly relieved by the thought that drugs would not be a problem. After all, the average resident was fifty-five , well-educated, retired, and generally not "into" anything other than birding, shelling, and leading a peaceful, law-abiding

life. The seashell island boasted no high schools, colleges, night life
or malls, and no federal agent ever dropped by to tell me we might
have a drug problem.

But while I wasn't wrong about the islanders, I was dead wrong
about the absence of a drug problem. For during the next few years,
the small SPD seized several tons of Mary Jane.

*   *   *

The Folks Back Home
Will Never Believe This!

In the seventies, numerous shrimp boats plied the waters of the
Gulf of Mexico. In theory, they were out there to catch tasty
crustaceans. In fact, many were already loaded with tons of "square
grouper" - bales of marijuana wrapped in Colombian newpapers and
covered with burlap.

Slowly wending its way up the west coast of Florida, a "mother
ship" with marijuana aboard would drop anchor off the shores of an
isolated area. Then, under cover of darkness, local fishermen - who
earned far more unloading Colombian dope than catching fresh
Florida grouper - would go out to meet the mother ship, off-load
some of its illicit cargo, and transport it to the mainland. The sheriff
of neighboring Collier County, home of the infamous fishermen of
Everglades City, nearly went out of his mind.

Clearly, it was impossible to monitor the nocturnal activities of
countless fishing boats from the Florida Keys to the Panhandle, for
local law-enforcement authorities had neither the equipment nor
manpower to mount such an operation. And while the *importation*
of illegal drugs was really a national rather than a state problem,
the federal government provided little (if any) assistance in the mid-
1970s. But sometimes, the good guys got lucky.

One Saturday night in April, 1977, the Florida Marine Patrol
trained a spotlight on a small flotilla of fishing boats. It immediately
became clear that the latter were carrying something far heavier
than fish, for their gunwales were just inches above the water.
While the officers boarded the first boat, the smugglers in the other

five dumped their non-piscatory cargo into the Gulf of Mexico.

Sunday morning, at the crack of dawn, a covey of devoted shellers made a beeline for Bowman's Beach in the hope of finding a rare specimen to add to their collections. But when they arrived, they found bales of square grouper worth infinitely more than rare shells. Fortunately, one disappointed sheller had the presence of mind to go to the nearest phone and call the police.

Shortly thereafter, the SPD arrived on a scene best described as chaotic. All along the shore, people were grabbing handfuls of marijuana from the beached bales. "The folks back home will never believe this!" said a happy fellow from Ohio, whose plastic shelling bucket was already full of Mary Jane.

While crowd control posed no problems, forty-eight bales of square grouper did. For since each bale weighed between forty and fifty pounds, we had to move a ton of marijuana off Bowman's Beach. However the SPD then had only a handful of sworn officers, one cruiser, one four-wheel drive, and no trucks.

Therefore, I called in our auxiliaries, and asked islanders who owned trucks if they would lend us a hand. As always, islanders were more than willing to help the SPD. Having resolved the problem of removing the marijuana from the beach, I now faced the problem of storing it. The SPD had moved three times in as many years, and currently occupied a portion of the fire station on Palm Ridge Road. Quite understandably, the Sanibel Fire Deparment (a separate taxing authority) took a rather dim view of sharing its quarters with us. Equally understandably, the fire chief expressed an unprintable degree of displeasure when the SPD stored a ton of Mary Jane in the inside area reserved for his flaming-red rigs.

I placated the fire chief by assuring him that our ton of marijuana was just a temporary inconvenience. The following day, the SPD would arrange to have the entire ton transported across the causeway to the Lee County Sheriff's Department in Fort Myers. Of course, I didn't tell the chief that it would probably take several days to get rid of all the dope. For since the sheriff's special compound for illegal drugs was already filled to capacity, he certainly wouldn't be the least bit interested in helping the SPD bring him any more.

Unlike the fire chief, I didn't fret over the marijuana that Sunday.

But on Monday morning, I became deeply concerned when I learned that three bales had mysterioulsy disappeared during the night. Therefore, and once again with the aid of auxiliaries and truck-owning islanders, I had the rest of the marijuana transported to the sheriff as soon as possible - whether he wanted it or not.

The SPD subsequently found the culprits who had pilfered the pot. However, the fact that we never recovered the missing bales became a source of considerable amusement for the local press - and embarrassment for the SPD.

*   *   *

The Pot Plot

The great hurricane of 1926 brought an abrupt end to commerical farming on Sanibel, for its extraordinarily high tides deposited salt all over the island. But by the mid-1970s, the salt had leached out considerably, and many islanders took great pride in their fruit and vegetable gardens. Perhaps inspired by the successful agricultural endeavors of adults, two teen-agers decided to become Future Farmers of America. But instead of growing oranges and eggplant, they grew pot - a far more profitable crop.

The boys turned out to be fine farmers. After clearing a small plot off Junonia Street, they planted their crop and tended it well. Indeed, they watered it regularly (bottled spring water, no less), and sprayed it with pest-control dust. But since gardening was not all that exciting, the boys began harassing a teen-age girl who lived near their pot patch. Thus, in October of 1977, the SPD received a complaint about the boys' behavior.

During the course of his investigation, Officer Ray Rhodes discovered the hallucinogenic garden of some thirty, thriving plants. He also saw the supply of bottled water and pest-control dust. But while Ray could follow up on the harassment complaint, he could not arrest the boys for growing the marijuana. For in order to make such an arrest, the police must catch suspects in the act of cultivating their crop.

Realizing the small SPD could ill afford either the time or manpower required to catch the young culprits in the act of cultivation, Ray devised a tactic that proved to be extremely effective. Accompanied by Officer Betty Weir, he returned to the pot patch the following week, and found that fifty more marijuana seedlings had been planted. Clearly, the boys had been very busy.

But since there are no laws against stealing or destroying illicit dope, the officers confiscated a few specimens (for educational purposes), trampled on all the rest, and left my calling card on a stump. The boys got the message.

* * *

Stumbling Lew

Exactly one year after the SPD demolished the little hallucinogenic garden, Officer Lew Phillips seized over 4,000 pounds of pot with a street value of nearly $2 million, and placed two smugglers under arrest. "Sanibel police stumble onto two-ton pot shipment," wrote a young island reporter. Not surprisingly, the long-haired latter considered members of the SPD incapable of finding any marijuana unless they saw it washed up on the beach or tripped over it in the mangroves. But although Phillips' fellow officers got a kick out of kidding "Stumbling Lew," they all knew the true story.

While patrolling the island during the dark hours of the graveyard shift, Lew drove through Sanibel Bayous shortly before dawn one Friday in the fall of 1978. Naturally, he didn't expect to see anything illegal going on in a remote subdivision that was largely undeveloped. But when Lew spotted two vans driving down Umbrella Pool Road without any lights on, he immediately became suspicious and decided to investigate.

After stopping both vehicles and asking for identification, Lew discovered that one man was driving without a license. Temporarily ignoring that relatively minor illegality, Officer Phillips asked him why they were driving in the dark without lights. "We were just looking for a good place to fish and got lost," he said.

Peering inside the first van, Lew didn't see any fishing poles; but he did smell the familiar fragrance of marijuana. In fact, the van was so tightly packed that the sliding cargo door remained partially open, and he could see piles of plastic and burlap bales. The same, telltale smell emanated from the other van, which was also loaded to the roof with the high-grade square grouper from Colombia.

Realizing that the police had caught them red-handed, neither smuggler made any attempt to resist arrest. Lew drove them to the SPD station, where we learned that 22-year-old Barry Alan Wheeler lived in West Palm Beach, and 26-year-old John Eric Hamm hailed from Lake Worth. But apart from revealing limited information, the smugglers proved to be singularly uncommunicative. Therefore, we soon transported the pair to the Lee County Jail, where they were booked for possession of over 100 pounds of marijuana, and conspiracy to import and deliver a controlled substance. Bond was set at $250,000 each.

While the smugglers were checking into Friendly Frank's Hotel, deputies from the Lee County Sheriff's Department were checking out the area around Sanibel Bayous. A few hundred yards from the spot where Stumbling Lew had stoppped the vans, they found a smashed pickup filled to the gills with square grouper. While the hapless driver was long gone, the LCSD believed that he had probably become disoriented while driving without lights - and crashed into a cabbage palm.

Then, since Officer Phillips' detailed report specified that the smugglers' blue jeans were wet and muddy up to the knees, the deputies combed the area around Old Blind Pass (which, in those days was still open). Their search uncovered evidence of recent unloading activity, which led the LCSD to surmise that a small skiff had entered the pass and dropped anchor near the waiting vans, whose drivers waded out to off-load the dope. But like the chauffeur, who presumably crashed into a cabbage palm, both the captain and his boat were long gone.

In any event, local newspapers really played up the smugglers' arrest and the seizure of a two-ton pot shipment. And, when I placed Lew's name in nomination for the Outstanding Public Service Award sponsored by the Fort Myers *News-Press*, islanders were delighted when he received it. Luckily, the newspapers didn't do a follow-up story on the fate of the smugglers, for the public would have been outraged to learn that they got off scot-free.

Wheeler and Hamm pleaded guilty, and never went to trial. Instead, since it was their first offense, the pair received a suspended sentence. However, I strongly suspected that, in return for such leniency, the authorities had extracted extremely valuable information. And since drug importers undoubtedly drew the same conclusion, they would never hire Hamm and Wheeler again. In short, the young men's smuggling days were over.

* * *

Chief Butler Wants a Boat

In addition to destroying commercial farming on Sanibel, the hurricane of 1926 sliced right through the neighboring island of Captiva and created Redfish Pass. As a result, "Upper" Captiva became a barrier island. Sharks used the pass as a shortcut, and so did smugglers en' route to Pine Island. But since the current was extremely strong and treacherous, the former held a distinct advantage over the latter - especially during a heavy storm. Such a storm occurred on the night of December 15, 1979.

Early the following morning, U.S. Customs called the SPD to report a beached boat on Upper Captiva. They had reason to believe it belonged to smugglers, who missed Redfish Pass during the storm, and asked if we would take them to the tiny barrier island. Although the SPD had no boat, I saw this as a golden opportunity to acquire one (for a smuggler's boat becomes the property of the law-enforcement agency that seizes it). Therefore, I told Customs we'd be delighted to transport them to Upper Captiva, and suggested they meet us at South Seas Plantation, the large resort on the Captiva side of Redfish Pass.

Despite the lousy weather, Captain Starr, the resort's dock master, readily agreed to take SPD and Customs officers over to Upper Captiva. But when we arrived, I was far less interested in looking for dope than in examining what I now considered to be the SPD's first boat. Unlicensed and bearing no identification numbers, the brand-new, twin-screw, 26-foot Wellcraft was beyond my wildest dreams! However, I dutifully joined the other officers, who were clearly more intent on following drag marks in the sand than admiring a beached boat.

The marks led to mangrove area, and over one ton of square grouper wrapped in Colombian newspaper and burlap. Some forty feet away from the bales of marijuana, we discovered two scruffy looking young men wearing heavy pea jackets and black stocking caps pulled down over their ears. Despite the blowing wind and bone chilling temperature, both were sound asleep. I shook the men awake, read them their rights, and placed them under arrest.

It immediately became clear that George Thomas Williamson and John Paul Baker had a great deal in common. Both were twenty-five-years-old, lived on Pine Island, and claimed to know nothing about either the Wellcraft or the 2,285 pounds of dope piled up so close to their sleeping quarters. They were just law-abiding mullet fishermen who, following the misfortune of having their skiff sink during a storm, had the good fortune to wash up on a barrier island.

In view of the overwhelming circumstantial evidence against the "mullet fishermen," we didn't think it was necessary to go through the time-consuming routine of obtaining concrete, physical evidence. Thus, we took no pictures of the beached boat, drag marks, or footprints. Nor did we confiscate the suspects' shoes (which matched the footprints), or clothes (which undoubtedly contained bits of marijuana). Indeed, we were so sure the SPD had an airtight case, and a new boat, that we spent little time interviewing the alleged smugglers. As it turned out, however, we lost both the boat and the case.

*   *   *

Capt. Starr brought us, the fishermen, and the marijuana back to South Seas, where we were met by a couple of deputies from the Lee County Sheriff's Department. The latter took custody of the suspects, and the resort kindly provided a large van to transport the square grouper to the sheriff's drug depot in Fort Myers.

Once the drugs were safely out of my hands, I focused on the problem of getting the Wellcraft to South Seas as soon as possible. The weather was rapidly turning from bad to worse, and I feared the boat would take quite a beating.

Fortunately, an SPD auxiliary agreed to bring over his own boat and pull the Wellcraft off the beach. During the process, however, the auxiliary's boat also became firmly embedded in Upper Captiva's beach. In desperation, I called a salvage outfit on Gasparilla - an island named after a legendary pirate.

Some time later, a salvage crew arrived. They soon freed the auxiliary's boat, and I breathed a sigh of relief when they subsequently pulled the Wellcraft off the beach. But instead of bringing the twin-screw to South Seas Plantation, the rescuers began towing it in the opposite direction! "Where the hell are you going with our boat?" I shouted over the ship to shore.

In reply, the rescuers from Gasparilla informed me they were taking the boat home because the sea was too rough to take it anywhere else. However, if the SPD really wanted it, we could pay a $3,000 salvage fee and pick up the boat at their home port, Boca Grande. Although the Wellcraft was well worth the ransom, I didn't have that kind of money in my budget in 1979 - and I knew the City of Sanibel was not in a position to provide it. But while the loss of the boat was disappointing, the loss of the case against the suspects was devastating.

Some six months after their arrest, the two mullet fishermen from Pine Island went to trial. Not surprisingly, and doubtless inspired by their lawyers, Williamson and Baker bore little resemblance to the disreputable-looking characters I had rudely awakened on Upper Captiva. In addition to being squeaky clean, freshly shaved, and nicely dressed, both men appeared in court with their loving wives and minor children. Duly impressed by such paragons of respectability, the jury found them not guilty.

Yet despite the loss of a seemingly open-and-shut case against two local mullet fishermen, the SPD succeeded in providing information that led to the seizure of the mother ship and its illicit cargo. For when we arrested Williamson and Baker in mid-December, we searched their tote bags and discovered several interesting documents. Among them were two passports (possibly those of friends who made it through Redfish Pass during the storm), and papers bearing the name of a shrimp boat, the *Carla Erickson.*

We immediately turned this information over to U.S. Customs. Shortly thereafter, the large shrimp boat loaded with thirteen tons of Colombian marijuana was seized off the shores of Sarasota.

* * *

Ms. Peterside Was Not Impressed

Soon after Officer Lew Phillips "stumbled" over two tons of marijuana in the fall of '78, I decided the SPD needed some night-surveillance equipment. Particularly, one pair of night-vision goggles that enabled one to see a considerable distance in the dark. Numerous law-enforcement agencies had found those goggles extremely effective in dealing with certain crimes that generally occurred at night.

Of course, such a splendid piece of surveillance equipment was extraordinarily expensive. And, in the late 1970s, Sanibel couldn't afford to pay nearly $10,000 for one pair of night-vision goggles. Therefore, I applied for a grant from the state's Bureau of Criminal Justice Assistance. Like most bureaucracies, the latter was well aware of the fact that the best defense is a good offense. Specifically, a barrage of paperwork requirements designed to discourage anyone from asking them for anything.

But since the SPD really needed a pair of night goggles, I complied with every one of the bureau's mind-boggling requirements. Thus, when I finally filed the SPD's application in the winter of '79, it included formal approvals of our request from the Regional Criminal Justice Board, the Planning Council, and the Florida Council on Criminal Justice. Unfortunately, Ms. Joyce Peterside, Chief of the Bureau of Criminal Justice Assistance, was not impressed.

Months later, Ms. Peterside informed me that she was withdrawing our request from consideration for the following reasons: Sanibel had no rapes, robberies, or murders in 1978; narcotics violations were "relatively minimal" in our area; the SPD didn't have enough sworn personnel "to receive the full benefits from the use of this type of equipment." In short, we didn't need any goggles.

I immediately fired off an epistle to Ms. Peterside, and indicated that copies were being sent to the Florida Council on Criminal Justice, the Division of Public Safety, Planning and Assistance, State Representatives Nuckolls and Mann, State Senators Childers and Lewis, and State Attorney Joseph D'Alessandro. If nothing else, I hoped that the names of all those VIPs would encourage Ms. Peterside to give my letter very serious consideration.

In all fairness to the Chief of the Bureau of Criminal Assistance, the facts outlined in her letter were correct. Sanibel had no reported cases of rape, robbery, or murder in 1978. And as far as narcotics were concerned, it was also true that "only 559 possessions violations" had been reported throughout the entire county. It was this statistic that caused the bureau chief to conclude that drugs were not a problem in Lee County in general, and Sanibel in particular.

Therefore, and as tactfully as possible, I explained to Ms. Peterside that the drug statistic she had cited was totally meaningless. For in those days, the statistics of the Uniform Crime Report (UCR) referred only to the *number* of people arrested for narcotics violations, and did not reveal the *volume* of narcotics involved. Thus, the UCR made no distinction between someone arrested for possessing one ounce of marijuana, and someone arrested for possessing one ton.

Having gained Ms. Peterside's undivided attention by demolishing the UCR's statistic, I immediately proceeded to court her favor with a heart-warming summary of the results of the SPD's valiant fight against illegal drugs. During the past four years, we had seized four-and-one-half tons of marijuana, four van-type vehicles, and a twenty-six-foot, twin-screw boat. The SPD had also had numerous drug-related arrests, and developed critical information that helped the Lee County Sheriff's Department make the largest cocaine arrest in the history of Southwest Florida.

However, Ms. Peterside's final objection to our application (not having enough personnel to use one pair of goggles), proved far more difficult to counter in a tactful manner. Therefore, I glossed over the fact that the goggles could only be worn by one person at a time, and enclosed an affidavit promising to let other law-enforcement agencies borrow the equipment.

Greatly to her credit, the bureau chief reconsidered our application, and the SPD subsequently obtained one pair of night-vision goggles.

* * *

Strange Seaweed

The eastern tip of Sanibel marks the entrance to the Gulf of Mexico from San Carlos Bay. While local tide charts persist in referring to it as Point Ybel, nearly everyone calls it Lighthouse Point. For in 1884, and doubtless to the delight of the proprietors and captains of cattle boats sailing to Cuba, the U.S. Government erected an iron lighthouse on ancient Point Ybel.

In view of its prime location and fine public beaches on both the Gulf and the Bay, Sanibel's eastern tip attracts scores of shellers, swimmers, sunbathers and beachcombers. But in mid-February of 1980, Lighthouse Point became a madhouse when hordes of people descended upon its shores and collected seaweed. However, the weed in question was not the kind of "gift from the sea" that Anne Morrow Lindbergh had in mind. Rather it was the remains of some twenty-one bales of marijuana.

The story of the strange seaweed began on a Thursday night, when the U.S. Coast Guard spotted the bad ship *Pipe Dream* off the shores of Fort Myers Beach. As the cutter closed in on the smugglers, the latter followed SOP (standard operating procedure), and started dumping their cargo into the Gulf of Mexico. But since it was impossible for three men to throw six tons of pot into the water on such short notice, the Coast Guard soon seized the *Pipe Dream* and the vast majority of its cargo.

Like all law-enforcement agencies, the Coast Guard was well aware of the monumental difficulties involved in seizing, hauling, storing, transporting, and destroying large quantities of square grouper. Therefore, and quite understandably, they didn't bother to pick up the bales the smugglers had tossed into the sea. Officially, the latter were chopped up by the *Point Steele's* propellers. Unofficially, the Coasties blasted them to smithereens with riot guns. However, neither the official nor unofficial method of destruction proved to be effective.

Shortly before sunset the next day, the SPD received a call from a concerned citizen who reported large clumps of marijuana washed up around the public fishing pier at Lighthouse Point. The officers who responded to the call quickly gathered the clumps into a dozen piles, and set them on fire. But while dealing with the seaweed situation that Friday night posed no problems for the SPD, it turned out to be little more than a dress rehearsal. For the following night pictures of Sanibel's hallucinogenic seaweed appeared on TV. As a result, legions of young people from Lee and neighboring counties descended upon Lighthouse Point early Sunday morning.

Like typical shellers, they carried plastic containers, kept their heads bowed, their backs bent, and their eyes riveted on the sand. However, it soon became apparent that the young people were not looking for rare yellow pectens, junonias, golden olives, or any other molluscan specimens. Instead, they were filling their containers with seaweed - specifically, the mind-boggling bonanza from the ill-fated *Pipe Dream*. Thus, the SPD had the dubious pleasure of chasing the weed seekers and raking up the pot.

Yet while our efforts were highly effective on Sunday, the problem didn't go away. Kids continued to flock to Lighthouse Point, for the tides kept bringing in more marijuana. But after days of chasing, raking, and burning, the SPD was greatly relieved to discover that the sea had finally exhausted its supply of pot from the *Pipe Dream*. By Wednesday afternoon, the tides yielded only sand, shells, real seaweed, and other legitimate gifts from the sea.

At the end of the four-day clean-up operation, our officer estimated that the SPD had confiscated and destroyed about fifty pounds of marijuana. Compared to the two tons seized by "Stumbling Lew" in '78 and the one ton we found on Upper Captiva in '79, fifty pounds appeared to be a piddling amount. However, it turned out to be the largest amount of marijuana we seized in the decade that had just begun - for Sanibel changed considerably during the 1980s.

Gulf-front properties that had once been relatively remote underwent rapid development. A condominium complex now lay within a stone's throw of Bowman's Beach and, much to the dismay of mullet fishermen, a severe storm closed Old Blind Pass. Many concerned citizens and devoted winter residents deplored the development of their "sanctuary island" - and so did marijuana smugglers. But instead of writing letters to the editor, the latter stopped coming to a developing area with a growing police department.

However, growth and development were not entirely responsible for the fact that the SPD dealt with ounces rather than tons of marijuana in the 1980s. For shortly after his inauguration, President Reagan declared war on drugs. Naturally, the Drug Enforcement Administration became extremely receptive to requests for assistance that poured in from sheriffs throughout Southwest Florida.

As a result, the sheriff of Collier County was delighted when federal agents arrested nearly everyone in Everglades City. The sheriff of Lee County was equally delighted when he no longer had to burn tons of Mary Jane in order to make room for more of the same.

Fifteen marijuana leaves and one coke leaf decals, displayed on the bridge of the 80' U.S. Coast Guard Cutter Point Steele, signifying drug vessels seized.

Shrimp boats at Fort Myers Beach.

The three vehicles were loaded to the roof with about two tons of marijuana.

Suspects John Eric Hamm and Barry Alan Wheeler leave Sanibel police headquarters on their way to the Lee County jail.

This pick-up loaded with marijuana was found smashed into a cabbage palm. The driver is still at large.

ISLAND REPORTER PHOTOS BY MARK WILLIAMS

Some young Sanibel gardeners were undoubtedly surprised this week when they found Police Chief John Butler's calling card in place of their carefully-cultivated marijuana plants.

ONLY YOUR HAIRDRESSER KNOWS FOR SURE

Soon after John Carter died, his wealthy widow decided that she would feel far more secure living in the crime-free Garden of Eden than the crime-ridden Garden State. Therefore, Jane Carter moved to Sanibel in 1974, and lived in a large, ground-level home on the shores of San Carlos Bay. For the next six years, she felt safe and secure.

Jane had no difficulty filling her time. She worked as a saleslady at Dotti of Sanibel, whose high-quality women's apparel attracted the kind of clientele the genteel Jane enjoyed meeting and assisting. Moreover, she had no difficulty filling her five-bedroom home on Isabel Drive. Indeed, it contained her most precious possessions: expensive paintings, priceless jade and ivory, every conceivable piece of sterling silver, and jewelry galore in dresser drawers.

Yet despite the enormous value of the items in her home, Jane Carter had no alarm system, no deadbolts on her outside doors, and no security locks on the sliding-glass doors by the swimming pool. A French poodle constituted her only protection. After all, no member of the Carter family had ever been the victim of a crime. And except for breaking into daytrippers' cars parked at public beach accesses, a criminal activity few islanders deplored, there was no crime on Sanibel.

But in the summer of 1980, Jane Carter became the victim of the first armed robbery committed in an occupied Sanibel residence.

*   *   *

Late in the afternoon of July 3rd, a small rental car created a large cloud of dust as it travelled along old Bay Drive, then an unpaved washboard road. After turning the corner, the driver pulled over and parked across the street from one of the boat docks along the canal. Two men emerged from the car, raised the hood, and walked around the corner to Jane Carter's house.

Had residents seen the cloud of dust, they would have thought nothing of it. People in the Sanibel Harbor subdivision were used to clouds of dust. Had residents seen the men from the rental car raise the hood, they would have thought nothing of that, either. On the eve of the Fourth of July weekend, rental cars poured onto the island and breakdowns were not uncommon. But since it was hot and muggy that Thursday afternoon, the few residents of Sanibel Harbor who had not gone north for the summer were inside their homes, with their doors and windows closed and air conditioners running full blast. Therefore, no one saw the culprits either coming or going.

The armed robbers went directly to the enclosed pool area behind the house, where they had no difficulty dealing with the screen door. Subsequently, they pried open the sliding-glass doors with a screwdriver and proceeded to ransack the residence. But while they snatched up numerous pieces of expensive jewelry, the bandits ignored the jade, the ivory, and the sterling silverware. Indeed, they were interested in only one thing: the diamond ring which, according to their friend, Gwen (not her real name), was somewhere in the house.

Frustrated by their failure to find the $250,000 ring John Carter had given his wife on their twenty-fifth wedding anniversary, the men decided to wait for Jane to return from work. They didn't have long to wait. Jane came home at 5:15, parked her car in the garage and, as usual, entered her home through the kitchen door. But what followed was not at all usual.

Instead of being greeted by her poodle, Jane Carter was grabbed by the masked men and pushed to the floor. Although the robbers removed all her jewelry, Jane wasn't wearing the ring they wanted. "Where's your big diamond ring?" they demanded. Jane was only too happy to tell them. In fact, she thanked God that the ring was in the house and not in a safe deposit box. Otherwise, she was convinced the men would have killed her.

Jane led the armed men from the kitchen to her bedroom (where, like so many people, she kept her valuables), and pointed to the dresser drawer that contained her anniversary ring. The excited robbers opened the drawer and rooted around, throwing pieces of gold jewelry on the bed until they finally found the diamond ring. They also found a pair of silk stockings, which they did not toss onto the discard pile on the bed. Instead, they used them to tie Jane's wrists together.

Before leaving, the masked men yanked out all the telepone lines in the house, shoved their victim onto a couch, and ordered her not to move for fifteen minutes. Although they pointed their revolvers at her for added emphasis, such terrifying tactics were totally unnecessary. By that time, Jane Carter was a basket case. Her only coherent thought was that her sister would soon arrive with the steaks they planned to have for dinner that night.

But as the minutes passed by and Carolyn failed to appear, Jane felt it was now safe to leave and seek help. She rushed over to the Kennedy home on Bay Drive, where her sister was "housesitting" for the summer. Finding no one there, she ran farther down the washboard road to the Leas' home. Quite understandably, the Leas called me rather than the SPD. After all, I lived right across the canal from them on Isabel Drive!

I immediately contacted our dispatcher, and directed him to send an ambulance and police officers to the Leas' residence. Although my wife and I had been enjoying a drink with an old friend, I told them I had to go out and didn't know when I'd be back. But while Betty was used to such announcements, the president of Mansfield's Emerson Electric was not. In fact, Hod Bolesky became so excited about the armed robbery that he insisted on going with me.

When we arrived at the Leas' a few minutes later, I realized that Jane Carter was on the verge of going into a complete state of shock.

Moreover, her wrists were so tightly bound that her hands had turned blue! Since my first concern was for the victim's welfare, it was extremely frustrating to waste precious time searching for a proper knife to cut off the painful silk stockings. As a result, I made a mental note to do something about this problem.*

During the brief period of time before the ambulance arrived, the highly distraught Jane Carter did her best to describe what had happened. Unfortunately, the information she provided was of little help. She told us to look for two white males of average height and average weight, perhaps in their late twenties or early thirties - a description that fit scores of men spending the holiday on Sanibel. Since Jane had not seen the getaway car, and the stick-up people were long gone, I knew there was no point in raising the drawbridge or setting up a roadblock.

When the ambulance came to take Jane to Dr. Wegryn's office on Sanibel-Captiva Road, I sent one of my men along with her. But I was running out of manpower. Auxiliary Pickens protected the scene of the crime, another man looked for evidence outside Jane's house, and I had to keep a patrol car on the road to respond to other calls for service. Since it was time to "do a neighborhood," all available manpower was called in.

If the public told the police everything they knew and observed, few crimes would remain unsolved. But in my experience, John Q. Public rarely reveals everything he knows unless the police ask him the right questions in the right manner and, above all, never make him feel that he might be required to testify in court. The answer to "Did you see the accident happen?" will probably be "No." However, a policeman might fill his entire notebook with the response to a less threatening question like "What happened here?" ("Well, the guy ran through the stop sign and crashed into that car over there with the water pouring out of the radiator and...")

Therefore, our officers who questioned residents of Sanibel Harbor that Thursday evening were trained to conduct interviews, not interrogations. Unfortunately, they didn't come up with any leads. For although islanders are generally extremely cooperative with the

---

* Subsequently, I issued knives to all members of the SPD. They came in handy for numerous things, especially cutting ropes on docks and boats.

police, especially when a crime occurs in their neighborhood, the fact remained that nobody had seen or heard anything unusual.

In the meantime, other members of the SPD worked the crime scene, searching for evidence both inside and outside Jane's house. In view of all the sand on Sanibel, we are sometimes able to find a good footprint. But since it was now raining, we had no luck on the outside. And apart from making an impression of the pry marks on the sliding-glass doors, we didn't come up with any evidence on the inside, either. Unfortunately, black fingerprint powder on Jane's white woodwork and light-colored furniture and carpeting constituted the most visible results of our fruitless efforts.

However, Jane Carter hardly noticed the black powder all over the place when I brought her home later that evening. While she refused to stay in the house Thursday night, Jane agreed to walk through the crime scene with me, a procedure that often helps victims recall important details. But after going through that painful ordeal, she was unable to add anything to what she had already told us. And since Jane had not worn her anniversary ring for quite some time, she couldn't think of anyone south of New Jersey who even knew it existed.

It was well past midnight when I finally returned to my home on Isabel Drive, dog tired and disappointed that hours of painstaking police work had failed to produce any leads. But above all, I was disturbed by the nature of the crime that had occurred. Armed robbery of an occupied residence violates a fundamental principle of our society: your home is your castle. If you can't be safe inside your own home, you can't be safe anywhere - not even if you live on the same street as the chief of police!

Since such depressing thoughts did nothing to improve my disposition, I've often suspected that my wife was even more delighted than I when the SPD began to break the case the following day, the Fourth of July holiday.

* * *

While "redoing" the neighborhood that Friday morning, I talked with Don Letter, a semi-retired dentist who lived just four houses away from Jane Carter. Don told me that around five Thursday afternoon, he had walked over to get a good look at a tan Chevette parked on Bay Drive. While the Chevette's presence didn't arouse his suspicion, it certainly piqued the interest of a man in the market for a small car! As a result, Don was able to give me a detailed description of the four-door hatchback bearing a Florida license plate and the name of a car rental company, possibly Budget.

Our next big break on Independence Day had nothing to do with luck, but everything to do with communication - specifically, information police receive from their contacts in the community. In the fictional world of the silver screen, police informants are invariably disreputable "snitches" who sell information. But in the real world, informants are just average citizens who want to help the police solve crimes (at no charge). Of course, an officer who is content to sit on his duff and drive around in a patrol car never makes any contacts. Fortunately, however, Ray Rhodes wasn't that kind of officer.

In addition to his many connections on the island, Ray had made some excellent contacts on the mainland while serving as an instructor at the Southwest Florida Police Academy. As a result, Agent Richard Chard, one of Ray's buddies in the Lee County Sheriff's Department, called Ray and told him what he had just heard from one of *his* friendly contacts at Frank's Bottle Club in Fort Myers.

According to Agent Chard's source, a local golf pro who was imbibing at the bottle club that Friday morning talked about a big diamond ring he had for sale. The pro drove a small car, lived in some condo on Sanibel, and his name was Bryan Caldwell. But Agent Chard's informant knew nothing about the woman who accompanied the prattling pro, except that her first name was Gwen.

In following up on Friday's leads, we learned that law-enforcement friends across the causeway suspected Caldwell of committing several robberies in the Cape Coral area. A check with Budget Rent A Car revealed he was driving a tan, four-door Chevette hatchback. Although the Budget people were also able to give us the car's license number, they didn't know which condominium Caldwell was staying in. And since there are hundreds of condos on Sanibel, I knew only too well that we would lose precious time checking all their parking lots.*

But on July 6, the SPD received further information from another friendly source: Caldwell might be staying at the Sundial. Officer Lew Phillips and Agent Chard immediately drove to the large complex on the shores of the Gulf of Mexico, named after a shell normally found on the shores of the Atlantic Ocean. However the officers had Caldwell rather than conchology on their minds that Sunday afternoon.

Although inquiries at the front desk revealed that Bryan Caldwell was not registered at the resort, the officers decided to check the lounge, which was open to the public. Lew discreetly asked one of the cocktail waitresses if she knew Caldwell, and she indicated a slender man in his late thirties seated at the bar. Perhaps sensing that he was being observed, the suspect soon left the lounge and walked down the street to the Sanibel Siesta Condominiums.

Lew and Agent Chard stopped Caldwell in the parking lot and, among other questions, asked him about Gwen. In no time at all, the golf pro claimed that Gwen was trying to frame him, and readily agreed to discuss the matter further at SPD headquarters. Followed by Phillips and Chard, the obliging Caldwell drove his Chevette rental car down to the station house next to the Three Star Grocery (now Pick Kwik). We read him his rights and indicated that we knew much more about the robbery than we actually did, whereupon Caldwell sang like a canary.

Since the purpose of misguided individuals who talk to the police is to save their own skins, their voluntary statements are almost invariably a mixture of fact and fiction. While the golf pro's deposition was no exception in this respect, it proved to be far more revealing than most. Once his statement had been typed up, even Caldwell realized how damaging it was and refused to sign it. By that time, it was too late. For whether he signed it or not, the state-

* People frequently call the SPD and ask us to locate a relative staying in "some condo on Sanibel." More often than not, the relative is driving a rental car (make and license number unknown to the caller), and staying in a condo listed under the owner's name. But even if the relative is driving his own car, and the caller can give us the license number, it takes one man a full day to check the parking lots.

ment could be used against him in court.

Although Caldwell's story turned out to be a real doozy, it began quite accurately. Gwen, a local hairdresser, looked after Sanibel Siesta Unit 209 while the owner was in Texas. Gwen gave the key to her boyfriend, John Kennedy, and told him he could stay in the apartment rent free. Since the condo had two bedrooms, Kennedy invited his friend Caldwell to share the freebie on the Gulf of Mexico. At this point, Bryan Caldwell was probably so busy dreaming up the rest of his story that he neglected to mention Kennedy's recent release from the state prison at Raiford.

In any event, and according to Caldwell, Gwen brought two handguns, two walkie-talkies, and three shoe boxes filled with jewelry to the condo on Thursday evening, July 3rd. Naturally, neither he nor Kennedy could resist touching the gold, pearls and diamonds the Sanibel hairdresser dumped out of the shoe boxes - especially the diamond ring "about the size of a nickel." After Caldwell and Kennedy had examined the expensive pieces of jewelry (i.e. left their fingerprints all over them), Gwen put the jewelry back in the boxes and stashed them somewhere in the condo. On Saturday, when Bryan was doing his laundry, he found the shoe boxes in the dryer. He removed the boxes and put them on the bathroom floor.

Q. "When you suspected that the jewels were 'hot items,' why didn't you contact the police?"

A. "It wasn't any of my business."

* * *

To search or not to search?

Although Caldwell had told us about all the jewelry in apartment 209, I realized that in this case obtaining a search warrant would be a highly problematical proposition. Preparing an affidavit involved several hours of work in Fort Myers, during which time I would have to assign two men to watch the condo (in case someone came back for the loot), and another man to keep an eye on Caldwell, whom we could not legally detain at that point.

But above all, I knew that any Lee County judge I woke up in the middle of the night was bound to take an exceedingly dim view of the fact that the SPD didn't know who owned apartment 209, didn't know who was in charge of it, and didn't have sufficient "probable cause" to search it. Therefore, we decided to go ahead and search the apartment without a warrant, and run the risk of having the evidence thrown out of court.

But like most professional policemen who find themselves in the unenviable position of making such damn-the-torpedoes decisions, I gave some thought to covering my assets. Fortunately, the cooperative Caldwell readily agreed to sign a form granting the SPD permission to search the premises of apartment 209 - except, of course, Kennedy's bedroom. As a result, we found the two guns, recovered all the stolen jewelry, and placed Caldwell under arrest for the armed robbery of Jane Carter.

However the small SPD had no holding cells, no evidence room, and no special area for impounded vehicles. Therefore, I had to make other arrangements for Caldwell, the recovered jewelry and the Chevette hatchback. Clearly, the golf pro would have to be transported to thè Lee County Jail. But since Friendly Frank's was twenty-five miles away, driving Caldwell to jail meant that the only police car then running at night would be off-island for over an hour.

Yet I was far more concerned about controlling the evidence than chauffeuring Caldwell, and with good reason. The police cannot enter any evidence into court unless they can prove it has been constantly under their control from the moment they discovered it. Therefore, I decided to store Jane's jewelry in the Bank of the Islands' vault. Had the vault been big enough, I would also have parked the Chevette there. But since it was not, we left the hatchback behind the Three Star Grocery, locked it, and sealed it with a considerable amount of evidence tape. Indeed, the impounded car looked more like an Egyptian mummy than a Chevette.

Islanders were very pleased with the results of the SPD's investigation. After all, Caldwell was now incarcerated in Friendly Frank's Hotel, Jane Carter's stolen jewelry had been recovered, and we had established continuous control over the evidence related to the armed robbery. However, I was well aware of the fact that the SPD would not possibly prevail in a court of law. In short, we didn't have a case.

The stolen jewelry, which Jane Carter could identify, constituted our only real evidence. Unfortunately, we found it on the bathroom floor, not in Caldwell's bedroom. Moreover, Jane could not identify the revolvers; nor could she identify either Caldwell or Kennedy, since both had worn masks. And although the SPD had discovered a screwdriver in Unit 209 that matched the pry marks on Jane's sliding-glass doors, its presence didn't prove that the suspects had used it to commit the crime.

Our hearsay evidence, the testimony of Agent Chard's source at Frank's Bottle Club, would certainly be thrown out of court. And our circumstantial evidence wasn't worth a continental, for Don Letter could not state for a fact that the impounded Chevette was the same car he had seen parked off Bay Drive. But worst of all, the SPD couldn't prove that Caldwell and Kennedy had ever entered the residence at 1314 Isabel Drive, for they left no fingerprints or footprints at the scene of the crime.

I realized that the only way the SPD could nail the golf pro and the ex-con was to prove "beyond a reasonable doubt" that they had broken into Jane Carter's home, stolen valuable items either by force or intimidation, and had no intention of ever returning those valuables to their rightful owner. But I also knew that without the full cooperation of Gwen, our chances of proving the preceding were nil. Therefore, we asked the Sanibel hairdresser to come to the police station, where we gave her the facts of life.

"Gwen, you're in deep trouble. Caldwell showed us the boxes of jewelry you brought to his apartment Thursday night. Guess what? Your fingerprints are all over them! And when we pick up your boyfriend, he'll tell us all about you. Now, we know you didn't stick up Jane Carter. Caldwell and Kennedy did. But since you helped them, we're going to charge you with armed robbery."

The SPD did not lie to Gwen. For it is indeed a fact that anyone who aids, abets, or procures another person to commit a crime may be prosecuted and punished as if he were the perpetrator of that crime. Doubtless aware of that fact, Gwen never questioned our right to charge her with armed robbery. But since the Sanibel hairdresser was no dummy, I knew she wouldn't take the rap for either the golf pro who had turned her in, or the ex-con who was currently turning her on. Therefore, in order to ensure her full cooperation, I decided it was time to throw Gwen a lifeline.

"There's only one thing you can do to save your own ass, Gwen: turn state's evidence. If you're willing to do this, we'll call the attorney who's handling the Carter case. And if he says okay, you can tell us everything you know and be home free."

Unlike Gwen, the prosecuting attorney knew perfectly well the SPD didn't have a case that would stand up in court. He readily agreed to give the hairdresser immunity in return for her testimony against Caldwell and Kennedy. And since Gwen had no desire to spend any time in jail, she told us the whole story.

* * *

After moving to Sanibel, Jane Carter used to have her hair done at the beauty parlor where Gwen worked as hairdresser. One day, when Gwen admired the large diamond ring her customer was wearing, Jane told her all about it. Indeed, she even held out her hand so the discriminating hairdresser could fully appreciate the magnificent diamond. As the time went by, Jane stopped wearing her anniversary ring, switched to another beauty parlor, and completely forgot about the friendly conversation with her former hairdresser. Unfortunately, Gwen did not forget it.

Thus, when Gwen became romantically involved with an ex-con fresh out of Raiford, she told her boyfriend and his golf-pro buddy about Jane Carter's rock of Gibraltar. Kennedy and Caldwell decided the ring was certainly worth stealing, whereupon Gwen drove them by Jane's home so they could case the joint. She also drove them by Dotti of Sanibel so they could look things over there as well.

While the men in her life were busy committing armed robbery and terrifying Jane Carter in the process, Gwen remained comfortably ensconced at the Sanibel Siesta condo. When the conquering heroes returned with their revolvers, the diamond ring, and other pieces of Jane's jewelry, they decided to celebrate their great victory by going out for dinner at 'Tween Waters Inn on Captiva. After all, they could certainly afford it.

Once Gwen had told us the whole story and signed an affidavit, I turned my attention to the man from Raiford. Ironically, John Kennedy had been sitting at the Sundial bar on Sunday afternoon and overheard Lew inquire about Bryan Caldwell and "a woman called Gwen." Realizing that it was only a matter of time until the police found out about him, the ex-con immediately left the island. He didn't even stop at the Sanibel Siesta condo to pick up either his personal possessions or any of the jewelry.

Several days later, the Lee County Sheriff's Department arrested Kennedy and escorted him to Friendly Frank's Hotel. I sent Officer Ray Rhodes over to have a little talk with him. Kennedy told Ray he couldn't stand the thought of spending any more time in prison, and wanted to play "let's make a deal" with the SPD. When the SPD said "no deal," the ex-con conned someone into guaranteeing the bond required to release him from jail before the trial. Not surprisingly, Kennedy jumped bond and vanished.

William Bryan Caldwell pleaded guilty. He was convicted of armed robbery and sentenced to thirty years in prison. Shortly after the trial, Jane Carter sold her lovely home on San Carlos Bay and moved to a residential community that provided on-site security twenty-four hours a day. But Jane never fully recovered from the terrifying experience she had suffered on Sanibel. Gwen, of course, didn't suffer at all. Having turned state's evidence, she was granted immunity from prosecution - and continued to work as a hairdresser.

Ten years later, little had changed. Caldwell was still in jail, Jane couldn't bear to talk about her ordeal, Gwen worked in a local beauty parlor, and John Kennedy remained at large. But in the spring of 1990, the long arm of the law reached out and touched him in the Lone Star State. In a desperate effort to avoid spending the next thirty years in prison, Kennedy wrote a letter to Officer Ray Rhodes and sent it to the SPD.

Of course, Kennedy had no way of knowing that the nice young officer who had visited him at Friendly Frank's in 1980 was now chief of police in a small Pennsylvania town outside Harrisburg. Thus, when the SPD received the letter requesting a statement from Ray Rhodes to the effect that Kennedy had merely been involved in

burglary rather than armed robbery, they placed a call to Pennsylvania.

Ray's response to Kennedy's incredible request was a model of
scatological simplicity: "This guy's gotta be shitting me!"

THE OLDEST
PROFESSION

Although the biologic urge assumes many forms, American society sanctions only one: sexual intercourse between a married couple, performed in a private setting. Since nearly everything else is illegal, the police are charged with the uneviable task of enforcing laws against bigamy and bestiality, incest and indecent exposure, prostitution and fornication, sodomy, pornography, adultery, etc.

While some "sex crimes" are serious (like rape, carnal knowledge of a juvenile, and intercourse with an insane female), the vast majority are misdemeanors. But few Americans are aware that obscene language is a misdemeanor. And few of Florida's thirteen million residents and forty million annual visitors know that only married couples who perform the sex act in the missionary position are legally entitled to pitch woo in the Sunshine State.

If the police enforced all the sex laws on the books, there would be no one left to run the store.

*　*　*

When I became Chief of the SPD in 1975, the average age of residents was fifty-five. While islanders were certainly not over the hill in terms of sexual drive, Sanibel offered nothing to stimulate it.

The seashell island boasted no bar featuring females dancing in an erotic manner, and no houses of ill repute. Wildlife slide shows and square dancing at the Community House, which served cookies and punch, constituted the most exciting forms of night life. Clearly, any hooker who crossed the causeway in the hope of setting up shop on this barrier island would go broke!

During the next ten years, Sanibel changed considerably. But the island remained essentially the same in several respects: it offered little night life, and the police had no "pussy posse." Thus, in 1985, I was unpleasantly surprised to learn that one of Sanibel's recent residents was a prostitute, actively engaged in selling both her body and cocaine.

In view of her dual occupations, the hooker/drug dealer undoubtedly did well on Sanibel. But an altercation with another woman, with whom she shared a home on Olga Street, soon changed all that. For the irate roommate called the SPD, and told us everything she knew about her former friend, Judy.

According to the roommate, Judy worked for a Fort Myers Beach escort service, whose employees provided a variety of services not listed in the Yellow Pages. Since both Judy and her employer had a vested interest in servicing as many customers as possible without undue delay, Judy kept a pager in her purse. She also, according to her enraged roommate, kept a supply of cocaine in a squeaky-clean place: a safe deposit box at Bank of the Islands.

After listening to the roommate's revelations and posing a few pertinent questions, Officer Ray Rhodes and Officer Rick Kennedy went to work. Rick called his wife and asked if he could bring a hooker home - all in the line of duty. Not surprisingly, Mrs. Kennedy denied that ourtrageous request. Rick then contacted one of his buddies, an airline pilot who owned a condo at Sand Dollar. The pilot gave the SPD permission to use his pad for such a delightful, line-of-duty purpose, whereupon Kennedy called the escort service on Fort Myers Beach.

Posing as an airline pilot on layover, Rick said that he'd like to spend the evening with a female companion. And since a friend of his had a great time with "Judy," Rick hoped she might be available.

The escort service assured the stranded pilot that Judy was indeed free that evening. But just for the record (should anyone be recording this innocent conversation), the service informed Rick that its girls provided *only* platonic companionship - and the fee was seventy-five dollars. Rick readily agreed, and a date with Judy was set for that evening at the Sand Dollar condominium.

Having made the arrangements, Rick and Ray came to me for funds to finance their on-going investigation. For like most police departments, the SPD received some money that never appeared in the annual budget. Such "buy money" enabled us to pursue certain sensitive cases (especially those involving narcotics), without making a formal request for additional funds - thereby alerting everybody and his brother that the police were about to make a drug bust.

With less than two hundred dollars left in our buy-money budget, I took a dim view of blowing it all on wining and dining a call girl, and dreaded explaining those expenditures to Sanibel's city manager. But my men managed to convince me that, like the goodness made famous by Mae West, wining and dining had nothing to do with it. And since a police chief must have confidence in the professional judgment of the officers he has trained, I gave Kennedy and Rhodes one hundred and seventy-five dollars in marked bills. As it turned out, my confidence was not misplaced.

* * *

Realizing that it was essential to eliminate the slightest suggestion of entrapment, Kennedy and Rhodes planned their operation very carefully. For if the case went to court, the SPD would have to prove that the prostitute solicited the policeman. Otherwise the call girl would claim that the policeman solicited her.

Bravely fighting back tears, she would assure the court that she didn't make a living doing such a dreadful thing. But she'd done it just this one time because she desperately needed the money to feed her children, pay her beloved grandmother's funeral expenses, whatever. Having confessed her crime, the hooker would suddenly burst into tears, whereupon nearly everyone in the courtroom would become convinced that the SPD was a bunch of heartless storm troopers.

In order to avoid such a scenario, Ray Rhodes hid in the bedroom closet when Judy knocked on the door of the Sand Dollar condo. Expecting to see an attractive, young woman standing on the threshold, Rick opened the door and was shocked to see a "real dog." Then in her early forties, Judy looked like she'd been used, abused, and around the track a few times. However, her low-cut dress revealed an outstanding pair of "hooters."

Once inside the condo, Judy got right down to business. Standing on one side of the kitchen counter, while Rick stood on the other, Judy recited her menu of sexual selections, their respective prices, and waited impatiently for the good-looking "pilot" to make up his mind. Rick told her he didn't want anything kinky ($500) - just conventional copulation.

"That's one seventy-five," she replied.

"One seventy-five! But the escort service told me it was seventy-five," protested the airplane pilot.

"It's seventy-five in Fort Myers, one seventy-five in Naples and Sanibel. Those are premium areas," Judy added by way of explanation.

Grumbling that he could save a hundred bucks by driving across the causeway, Rick reluctantly agreed to pay the outrageous price of a one-night stand on Sanibel.

"Will that be cash or charge?" asked Judy. For like most prostitutes, she wisely insisted upon full payment in advance. As if to emphasize that point, she removed a small machine from her purse and explained that it was programmed to accept all major credit cards.

Sensing some hesitation on the pilot's part, Judy quickly assured him that his sexual activity on Sanibel would be billed as a dinner at an Italian restaurant on Fort Myers Beach. His wife would never know the difference.

"Cash," said Rick, handing the hooker the SPD's marked money.

Judy quickly counted the bills, shoved them in her purse, and made a beeline for the bedroom. She immediately stripped, perched provocatively on the bed, and urged the pilot to hurry up and get on with it. After all, her livelihood was largely dependent on in-and-out deals, no more than thirty minutes per customer.

At this point, Kennedy expected Ray Rhodes to pop out of the closet and place Judy under arrest *before* she began her illicit act (an important, legal consideration). But since Ray remained in the closet, Rick slowly removed his shirt - hoping like hell his partner would soon appear. The latter did not, however, because he was having a good time giving him a hard time.

Now extremely nervous, the unsuspecting Kennedy bent over to remove his shoes. "I'm now taking off my right shoe!" he announced in a stentorian voice his partner could not fail to hear.

Although puzzled by the pilot's pronouncement, the hooker became concerned when her customer began to giggle. "Hey, what's going on here?" she asked with mounting suspicion. In response, Ray Rhodes burst out of the closet.

"Oh, I get it," said Judy, who thought she now had two customers - until Ray told her she had none.

* * *

While Judy was cooling her heels at Friendly Frank's Hotel, the SPD ran a check on her and came up with several prior arrests for prostitution in the Peach State. But since hookers routinely get off with little more than a judicial slap on the fanny, I was far more interested in nailing the head of the escort service and exposing Judy's alleged involvement with drugs.

Unfortunately, the pimp had already covered his assets by re-quiring his dozen-plus employees to sign affidavits stating that they would not prostitute themselves. Moreover, and like most call girls, Judy feared retaliation and refused to testify against her employer.

Not surprisingly, she also remained silent on the subject of drugs. As a result, the SPD didn't have sufficient probable cause to obtain a search warrant for her safe deposit box. However, Judy made a monumental mistake.

"If you're guilty, go before a jury," is a gem of jailhouse wisdom. In fact, courtroom lawyers frequently offer their guilty clients the same advice. For unlike judges, juries are highly unpredictable. But since Judy was far more interested in getting back to work than waiting for a jury to find her innocent - or fine her fifty dollars - she went before a judge.

The latter proved to be singularly unsympathetic. He ordered her to perform all kinds of community service, and fined her a thousand dollars! Judy appealed the judge's decision, and lost once again.

Delighted by the final outcome of his operation, Officer Kennedy never dreamed the hooker would haunt him for several years. But just a few months after Judy lost her appeal, Rick received a long-distance call from Tallahassee. It soon became apparent that the practitioner of the oldest profession had applied for a teaching position in the public schools.

Yet although the Department of Education in one of the nation's fastest-growing states desperately needed teachers, it tried to avoid employing people whose morality left something to be desired. Rick informed the DOE that Judy's morality left a great deal to be desired. The hooker was not hired, and the SPD received no further inquiries or complaints about her. As it turned out, however, Judy had not disappeared from the scene.

The following spring, some 6,000 people descended upon the Dunes Golf & Tennis Club for one of Sanibel's most popular events: Taste of the Islands. As usual, the SPD was out in force to direct traffic, maintain order, and prevent people from parking in the special places reserved for sponsors and VIPs. Thus, when a stretch limousine pulled up in front of the clubhouse, Officer Jim Wilson politely opened the door for the VIP passenger.

Wearing a dress designed to reveal rather than conceal her humongous hooters, Judy stepped out of the limousine. She smiled at the wide-eyed Wilson, and proceeded to stroll around the spacious grounds. Not surprisingly, the SPD officers on duty at the Dunes got a good laugh out of Judy's appearance at a charitable fundraiser for the benefit of Care and Rehabilitation of Wildlife.

But Officer Rick Kennedy was more troubled than tickled by the hooker's triumphant return to Sanibel. For if Judy's procurer was having her chauffeured to "prime areas" in his pimpmobile, the escort service must really be booming! And indeed it was.

Some months later, the police in neighboring Collier County (home of the "prime" city of Naples), arrested the big-time procurer who operated *several* escort services: Judy.

* * *

Although Judy held the dubious distinction of being the only hooker arrested during my years with the SPD, others undoubtedly practiced their profession on the seashell island. But since they maintained a very low profile (and those blessed with both great bodies *and* post-graduate degrees commanded enormous fees), Sanibel's high-class hookers posed no problems.

However, male exhibitionists were a problem that defied solution. For unlike professional prostitutes, "wienie waggers" thrive on high visibility. Indeed, they can only perform in public. But since indecent exposure is a misdemeanor the *police* must see, the SPD was rarely able to cite a wienie wagger for violating State Statute 800.03.

Quite understandably, most women who called to complain about an unpleasant experience with an exhibitionist could not understand why we didn't rush right out and arrest "that horrible man." But on Sanibel, the typical exhibitionist does not hang around shopping centers and fling open his raincoat when the crown jewels are at the height of their glory. Instead, he takes full advantage of the sub-tropical climate and, minus the raincoat, heads for the beach.

When he spots a female who strikes his fancy, the exhibitionist masturbates, approaches the woman, and exposes his erection. Tah-dah! The hapless victim is always shocked, and often shrieks - reactions from which exhibitionists derive sexual satisfaction. Rare indeed is the woman who can laugh at a wienie wagger, an unexpected reaction that causes instant deflation of the latter's pride and joy.

In any event, most exhibitionists were smart enough to leave the beach after shocking some poor lady out of her wits. Thus, we rarely found a man who matched the complainant's description in the area where the misdemeanor occurred. And even if the complainant pointed to a man and said, "That's the one!" we couldn't arrest him for a sex crime the police didn't see him commit. All we could do was have a little chat with him.

But while complaints about exhibitionists were a frequent cause of frustration at the SPD, "The Case of the Chinese Chef" boosted morale considerably.

*   *   *

One fine morning, someone from Bailey's General Store called to complain about a man who was exposing his genitals. Since I happened to be driving around the area in plain clothes, I told the dispatcher I'd handle the call.

When I arrived at Bailey's, the complainant pointed to a China-man sitting on one of the benches outside the store. "Every time a woman walks by, the damn Chink starts masturbating," he grumbled. "You've gotta arrest him, Chief — this sort of thing is bad for business!"

While I had to agree with the complainant, I also had to see the accused make a willful, indecent, and public exposure of his "person" in a manner either offensive or annoying to those present. Otherwise, I couldn't arrest him. But since there was no way I could inspire the accused to expose his person, I decided to hang around and wait for a woman to walk by. Fortunately, I didn't have long to wait.

Within minutes, a van from one of the resorts pulled in and a group of maids poured out. When the women approached the store, the Chinaman began flogging his bishop - and continued to do so until I tapped him on the shoulder and arrested him for indecent exposure. I then drove the accused to the station for booking, and he was later transported to the Lee County Jail.

While at the station, the Chinaman told us he was gainfully employed as a chef at a resort on neighboring Captiva Island, and had never been in trouble with the law. Since both statements turned out to be true, I derived no comfort from the fact that the SPD had finally succeeded in catching and incarcerating a wienie wagger. For in my opinion, our prize catch would probably spend one night in Friendly Frank's Hotel, and be released in time to prepare Peking Duck at the Captiva resort the following day.

Like most people, I don't enjoy being wrong. But in the Case of the

Chinese Chef, I was delighted to learn that I was dead wrong. Further investigation of the prisoner revealed that he was an illegal alien. As a result, he was transported to Miami, and allegedly deported by the U.S Immigration and Naturalization Service.

I often wondered how the chef explained his trouble with the law to the folks back home.

DIAMONDS AREN'T A GIRL'S BEST FRIEND

The most expensive raw material on earth, diamonds are also the most durable natural substance known to man. Thus, according to centuries of tradition, a fine diamond imparts a kind of invulnerability to its possessor. In fact, however, a fine diamond renders its owner highly vulnerable. Indeed, Louis XIV's Hope Diamond became history's most infamous gem when a series of subsequent owners were murdered, "accidentally" killed, or committed suicide. Fortunately, the last owner had the good sense to donate the diamond to the Smithsonian.

Not surprisingly, saleslady Sheila Lankin had clients rather than cursed diamonds on her mind when she arrived at Seagull Estates on January 9, 1985. Scheduled to "sit" the new subdivision off West Gulf Drive that Wednesday, Sheila's job involved welcoming people who wandered into the office, the Pelican model home, and showing the adjacent Sandpiper and Egret models to those who filled out a short registration form. During the house tour, Sheila would do her best to persuade prospective buyers that a residence in Seagull Estates, "a home to resort to," was well worth a quarter of a million dollars.

However, the forty-seven-year-old saleswoman was well aware of the fact that few of her "walk-ins" would be prospective buyers. For like all experienced real estate agents, Sheila knew that some people stop by model homes to get decorating ideas, others like to indulge in wishful thinking, a number come out of curiosity, and many appear simply because they can't think of anything else to do with themselves or their high-season houseguests.

Sheila Lankin was fully prepared to cope with all of the preceding at Seagull Estates. But the saleslady didn't stand a chance against the walk-in who hit her on the head, fired two shots into her back, and left her to die on the floor of the Egret model.

*   *   *

Alas, Sheila Lankin was dead by the time Neil Schoonderwoerd found her lying in a pool of blood on the bedroom floor. A former policeman, the sales manager did not forget his training. He immediately informed the two customers who followed him into the Egret model that he had a medical emergency and they would have to leave. As soon as the bewildered clients departed, Neil raced back to the office and called the SPD. It was now two forty-five.

I was off duty that fateful afternoon when the dispatcher called me at home and relayed the report of "a possible homicide" at Sea-gull Estates. Thus, I arrived at 523 Daniel Drive shortly after the personnel from the Medical Examiner's Office. But as soon as I stepped inside the model home, I realized that the possible homicide was a definite homicide. For death has a distinctive odor - indescrib-able, yet unmistakable to those who have frequently been exposed to it.

The sequence of events became all too clear as I walked through the crime scene. Blood on the dining room table, in the hallway lead-ing to the master bedroom, and on an artificial plant near the bathroom indicated that the killer had struck Sheila in the dining room and forced her into the bathroom off the master bedroom. Blood on the mirror, counter, sink, and faucet (still running), and a spent bullet on the floor left no doubt that the victim had been shot in the bathroom. Indeed, the lower part of her body lay in the bath-room, and the large pool of blood proved that the mortally wounded saleslady had not died immediately.*

---

* Powder burns indicated that the victim had been shot at point-blank range, pos-sibly by a left-handed person.

Three blood-stained articles lay close to Sheila Lankin's body: a pair of aviator-type sunglasses, a Seagull Estates sales packet, and a piece of pink, shell-shaped soap. Not much for us to go on. However, a sharp-eyed medical examiner noticed a band of white skin on the victim's ring finger, a clear indication that the tanned saleslady usually wore some kind of ring.

If the ring had been hard to remove, that would explain the soap and the running water. But if robbery were the motive for murder, I wondered why the killer had not taken the victim's gold bracelet and earrings as well. Perhaps the ring was so valuable that the killer simply didn't care about the other jewelry. On the other hand, the saleslady might not have been wearing the ring.

My thoughts were interrupted when Officer Ray Rhodes brought me several items the deceased had left at the office in the Pelican model: her real estate papers, purse, and the registration forms of people who had visited Seagull Estates that day. Since there was no point in doing a neighborhood (the new subdivision had only three model homes and no residents), I drove to the station, turned over the items to be tagged and placed into evidence, and concentrated on solving the most vicious crime that had ever occurred in the history of the SPD.*

* * *

Oddly enough, murder is generally one of the easiest crimes to solve because the killer is often someone the victim knew. In fact, the police frequently arrive at a crime scene and find the killer still standing there with a smoking gun, a bloody knife, or whatever other weapon he used. And more often than not, the murderer volunteers the information that he just killed so-and-so.

---

* The police must be able to prove that every piece of evidence they find has been continuously under their control from the moment they discovered it. Otherwise, it will probably be thrown out of court. Therefore, a designated "evidence person" is assigned the enormous responsibility of tagging and keeping track of all physical evidence. In this case, that critical task was entrusted to Officer Janet Cali, assisted by Officer Wayne Hinz. Their performance proved to be so outstanding that the Assistant State Attorney subsequently informed me that he owed them "a particular debt of gratitude."

But since Sheila Lankin's killer didn't fall into that category, and left no clues to his identity, I knew we were going to need all the help we could get from the general public. Therefore, I decided to inform the media of our predicament in the hope that some citizen would come forward with vital information.

Of course, I realized that publicizing a heinous crime during the height of the tourist season might not please the Sanibel-Captiva Chamber of Commerce. But having made the decision to do so in order to solve the crime, I turned my attention to more pressing matters that Wednesday afternoon. Specifically, interviewing Sheila Lankin's son and her live-in boyfriend. Quite understandably, both men were extremely upset.

It immediately became clear that Jerry Lankin thought the SPD was a pissant police department. Frustrated and angry, he asked me to get some "real policemen" to come over and find the person who killed his mother.

Naturally, I was sorely tempted to inform the young man that I was by no means a Mickey Mouse policeman. After all, I'd attended a special homicide school at the Southern Police Institute, and had never had an unsolved murder during my eighteen years as a police chief - eight in an industrial city that had its share of murders.

But since a professional police officer who allows his emotions to get the better of him risks losing both respect and cooperation, I didn't tell Jerry Lankin any of the above. Instead, I told him the only truth he wanted to hear: the SPD would certainly seek the help of other law-enforcement agencies, including the FBI.

Calmed by such assurances, Jerry Lankin became extremely cooperative. After examining the sunglasses found at the scene of the crime, he said they didn't belong to his mother. And when I asked Jerry if his mother normally wore a ring, he told me she wore a rather large diamond ring and *never* took it off.

Interviewing Sheila Lankin's live-in lover proved to be far more difficult than interviewing her son, for Ron Levy was in a state of shock when he arrived at the station. Although I felt like shaking him to his senses, I didn't want to lay myself open to a charge of "police brutality." Therefore, I supplied quantities of Kleenex and waited for the grief-stricken man to calm down. When he finally gained control of himself, Ron Levy did his very best to provide information that might help us find the murderer of the woman he loved.

Like Sheila's son, Ron said the aviator-type sunglasses did not belong to the deceased, and confirmed the fact that she always wore her diamond ring. He also told us that Sheila was a very feisty woman who would never have surrendered it without putting up a fight. But unlike Jerry Lankin, Ron Levy came up with the names of two people who might be suspects: specifically, her former boyfriend, John (Jack) Kornbluth, and her former employer, Josef Wojcie-chowski.

Although it was Kornbluth who gave Sheila Lankin the large diamond ring she never removed, Ron told me the two were no longer on friendly terms. In fact, Sheila had recently flown to California and testified against her ex-boyfriend in court concerning property she claimed belonged to her and not to him. And according to Ron Levy, Sheila had also been calling a host of government agencies in connection with a $3,500 claim against her former employer, Josef Wojciechowski of ZJ European Homes.

It occurred to me that if the saleslady's past activities were at all similar to her recent activities, there might be more than two people with motives for murdering her.

* * *

It was nearly sunset by the time I finished interviewing Lankin and Levy. But since it was still afternoon in California, I succeeded in contacting the attorney who handled Sheila's lawsuit against Kornbluth. Fortunately, the first of many long-distance calls the SPD made in connection with the Lankin case proved to be highly productive.

Attorney Henry Starr filled me in on the details of Sheila's lawsuit, informed me that Kornbluth was currently residing in the Dominican Republic, and gave me the suspect's telephone number. Thus, on the night of the murder, Officer Ray Rhodes placed a long-distance call to the Dominican Republic.

Jack Kornbluth told Ray that the three-carat, heart-shaped diamond he'd given Sheila Lankin was mounted on a wide, gold ring and worth about $10,000. From this description, Officer Lew Phillips, a highly talented artist, was able to draw a sketch of the ring. Regrettably, the press subsequently described the stolen ring as a four-carat, pear-shaped diamond worth anywhere from $20,000 to $80,000.

Officer Rick Kennedy was also busy making telephone calls on the night of the murder. Assigned the tedious task of contacting people who had filled out Sheila Lankin's registration forms that day, Rick persevered until he succeeded in reaching every one of them. Yet while all were cooperative, none could provide any information that might lead to the arrest of the individual who had shot the saleslady between 1:00 and 1:30 P.M.

But soon after the local TV stations reported the murder and the SPD's appeal to the public on the evening news, we received numerous calls. Surprisingly, none were crank calls from individuals who get their jollies by sending the police on a wild goose chase or confessing to crimes they didn't commit.

The vast majority of callers were people who had visited, driven by, or been in the vicinity of Seagull Estates that day and hoped the information they provided would help us solve the crime. Yet despite their good intentions, only one caller had information that might forward the investigation.

Louann Good, a Sanibel real estate agent, reported that she had driven by Seagull Estates around one o'clock that afternoon and had seen only one car parked at the office (the Pelican Model). Since salespersons make a point of checking the number of cars at open houses held by their competitors, there was every reason to believe that Louann Good's car count was accurate. But apart from describing the automobile as celery-green and possibly a BMW, she couldn't tell us anything more about the only vehicle she spotted at Seagull Estates.

I finally returned to my home that Wednesday night, painfully aware that we had almost nothing to go on. I also realized that Thursday morning's newspaper coverage of the brutal murder of a Sanibel real estate agent would send shock waves from Lighthouse Point to Blind Pass. For in one way or another, one out of five islanders is involved in real estate.

In the age of instant gratification, Sanibelians would expect the police to capture the killer immediately. Thus, for the second time in my life, I prayed to the good Lord to help me find a murderer.

Thursday January 10

Around eight-thirty, Officer Wayne Hinz received a call from a man vacationing in Fort Myers who identified himself as Robert Burton from Nashville, Tennessee. The latter said that he'd just read the morning newspaper and wondered why the police hadn't called him about the murder of Sheila Lankin.

Not knowing whether he was dealing with a concerned citizen or a certifiable kook, Wayne asked Mr. Burton why the SPD should have contacted him. "Because," he calmly replied, "I was probably the last person to see her alive."

Of course, the murderer would have been the *last* person to see Sheila Lankin alive. But Wayne wisely refrained from asking the caller if he were the killer. Instead, Officer Hinz asked him if he would mind coming over to the station and telling us his story. Burton readily agreed, and arrived about an hour later. I soon realized that Robert Lipscomb Burton, Jr. was the kind of witness who comes along once in a lifetime.

A man in his late forties, Robert Burton was intelligent, articulate, and remarkably observant. He told us that he'd arrived at Seagull Estates around twelve forty-five the previous afternoon, parked his bicycle at the Pelican model, and walked into the office. Sheila Lankin greeted him, and they discussed the new subdivision for a little while until a young man entered the sales office. Shortly thereafter, both Burton and the other walk-in filled out a registration form, whereupon the saleslady gave them brochures and took them on a tour of the Sandpiper and Egret models.

At approximately one-twenty, Robert Burton decided that he'd seen all he needed to see and thanked the saleslady for the tour. Since all three then headed for the Egret's front door, he assumed the other customer had reached the same conclusion. However, Burton soon realized that such was not the case. For as he started out the door, he heard the young man ask the saleswoman more questions about the home.

Burton returned to the office, got on his bike, and glanced back at the Egret model. Sheila Lankin and the young man were not on the front porch, nor were they on the path leading to the office.

But Robert Burton wasn't at all surprised that Sheila and the other customer were still inside the house. For throughout the tour, the latter had talked a great deal, asked numerous questions, and appeared to be knowledgeable about real estate. Nor did Burton find it the least bit odd that the young man periodically wandered off on his own during the tour.

However, sheer curiosity prompted the gentleman from Nashville to pay particular attention to the other walk-in. For Robert Burton kept wondering how such a young man could possibly afford to buy property in Seagull Estates.

During the course of the house tour, the talkative walk-in revealed a considerable amount of personal information. He said he was married, had several children, and currently lived on Fort Myers Beach. His wife was looking for property in Fort Myers, they owned land in Cape Coral, and wanted to live in a two-story house.

He inquired about local schools, asked if the gazebo went with the Sandpiper, and whether hardwood floors were included in the price of the Egret. Since the young man punctuated this last question by stamping his foot on the floor, Burton looked down and noted that his fellow walk-in was wearing gray shoes.

When I asked Burton if he'd seen a celery-green BMW parked at the Pelican model, he replied that the car in question was definitely not a BMW and proceeded to draw a sketch of the vehicle's front bumper and headlights. But realizing that the police would want more information than he could provide, the middle-aged man asked whether the SPD had contacted the young man from Fort Myers Beach. Wayne Hinz told him that we had not, because the police found no registration card for anyone from Fort Myers Beach. In fact, he added, the SPD found no registration form for Robert Burton, either.

I had a gut feeling that the man from Nashville was telling the truth. For had he not called us, we would never have known about Sheila Lankin's last two customers. Since my top priority was to find the other walk-in, we needed a good physical description of the subject. Robert Burton gave us a detailed description of the six-foot, thirty-year-old, white male from his Prince Valiant haircut to his light-gray shoes.

Thanks to Burton's complete description, a member of the Lee County Sheriff's Department was able to make a composite drawing. I put out a news release requesting information anyone might have about the suspect or his car, and drew up a flyer for distribution to some three hundred realtors in the Fort Myers area.

Other SPD officers contacted Sanibel's several dozen real estate agencies, provided the suspect's description, and secured the names of all salespersons who had been "babysitting" model homes the day of the murder.

Since every member of the SPD was working on the case, we began to rack up a lot of overtime. Quite understandably, taxpayers take an exceedingly dim view of overtime. After all, public servants should not pad their paychecks by persisting in doing today what they can perfectly well do tomorrow.

But since the clock starts ticking from the time a crime is committed, time is always of the essence in police work. For every minute that passes increases the criminal's chances of escaping apprehension. Therefore, it's impossible for any police department worth its salt to postpone until tomorrow what must be done today.

Forturnately, the SPD's overtime efforts soon paid off.

Friday January 11

First thing in the morning, Officer Ray Christensen received a call from Sanibel saleslady, Kathy Orwick. Kathy told him that after hearing a TV newscast, she realized the man who had recently visited Bayside Village fit the description of the person the SPD wanted for questioning.

In pursuing this promising lead, Ray learned that a young man with a helmet-style haircut had registered at the subdivision on Tuesday, returned on Wednesday morning (the day of the murder), and asked for "Pam," the saleswoman who had greeted him the previous day. But when Kathy informed him that Pam was not on duty that morning, the young man became visibly upset and left abruptly.

In addition to telling Ray everything she remembered about the young man, Kathy gave him the registration form the suspect had filled out at Bayside Village. It listed a telephone number, an address on Fort Myers Beach, and was signed by Markham William Dowell. Although the address and phone number were false, the name was not. As a result, Officer Wayne Hinz traced Dowell to his home in Cape Coral and called him around 10:00 A.M.

From the very beginning of what turned out to be a long day with Mark Dowell, Wayne gained the latter's confidence and cooperation by approaching him in a friendly, non-threatening manner. Thus, when he called Dowell that morning, he didn't greet him with the news that the SPD wanted to talk to him about the murder of Sheila Lankin. Instead, Wayne told him that he was just doing a routine follow-up investigation and had received information that Mark had visited Bayside Village on Tuesday. Was that information correct?

Mark readily agreed that it was. And when Wayne asked Dowell to describe himself and his car, Mark didn't hesitate to tell him that he was twenty-nine, about six feet tall, had a "bowl type" haircut and drove a medium-green Audi. But in response to other questions, Dowell maintained that he'd not been anywhere on Sanibel on Wednesday and never visited Seagull Estates. Since Wayne's primary purpose was to encourage the suspect to talk to the SPD, he didn't challenge those replies. Thus, Mark agreed to come over to the island as soon as his wife returned home with their car.

While Wayne was busy talking to Dowell, I finally managed to track down Sheila's former employer, the second of Ron Levy's suspects. When I subsequently interviewed Josef Wojciechowski at the station, he appeared to be totally unaware that Sheila Lankin had tried to cause him any financial problems.

Moreover, like Jack Kornbluth, Ron Levy, and Jerry Lankin, the man from ZJ European Homes had a good alibi. But since no alibi is "good" until the police have verified it, all of the preceding remained suspects in the eyes of the SPD. In fact, even the forthcoming Robert Lipscomb Burton, II, fell into that category.

Soon after Wojciechowski and his wife left the station, Dowell and his wife arrived with their two-year-old son. For the next half-hour, Wayne and Ray Rhodes interviewed Mark while I interviewed Vicky, and SPD Secretary Betty Balph babysat the toddler. But although both parents proved to be cooperative, their child refused to follow suit. As a result, my long-suffering secretary subsequently reported that the toddler was "acting like a real monster." But thanks to Betty Balph, I was able to talk to the toddler's mother without interruption.

During the course of our conversation, I concentrated on finding out as much as possible about the young couple: family and educational background, reasons for moving to the Fort Myers area, financial situation, etc. In short, I was fishing for any information that might explain *why* Markham William Dowell had now become the prime suspect in the murder of a total stranger. But since my questions were non-threatening in nature, Vicky Dowell didn't hesitate to answer them - and we both laughed about the fact that she was born on Christmas Day.

While interviewing Vicky, I soon realized that the young Dowells didn't fall into the category of deprived, destitute, desperate or depraved individuals, generally called "the criminal element." Born into America's middle class (Mark's father was a doctor and Vicky's father owned a construction firm), both were high-school graduates with some college education.

The couple had been happily married for three years, had no financial problems (Dr. Dowell regularly sent them stock), and they planned to open a day care center in Fort Myers. Their respective families were delighted with the marriage and, according to Vicky, Mark was a good provider and "a very likeable guy."

Vicky did her best to make it appear that the Dowells were the personification of that wholesome American myth, the Norman Rockwell family. But since policemen believe in neither myths nor appearances, I began to ask more probing questions.

Did Mark own a gun? Vicky said he did, but she had no idea where it was. It might still be packed away with other belongings the Dowells managed to save from a fire that broke out when they were staying at the Lighthouse Resort on Fort Myers Beach. I then asked if Mark had any gray shoes, and Vicky assured me he did not. Fortunately, Mark told Officers Hinz and Rhodes much more than his wife told me.

* * *

When Ray Rhodes brought Mark into the investigation room, Wayne Hinz introduced himself as the officer who had telephoned him and prepared to read the suspect his rights. But before he could proceed with that essential, legal formality, Dowell volunteered the information that he'd lied to Wayne. Specifically, Mark admitted that he *had* visited Seagull Estates on Wednesday and left his sunglasses at the scene of the crime!

Though doubtless stunned by Dowell's admission, Wayne had the presence of mind to read the Miranda Warning before the suspect made any more spontaneous statements that couldn't be used against him in court. Mark stated that he fully understood his rights, signed a waiver form, and never requested an attorney at any time during the interview. After all, a clever fellow who could talk his way out of anything didn't need a lawyer to keep him from talking his way into jail.

Dowell began by saying that he'd seen the news on TV Thursday night and immediately knew he was the person the police wanted for questioning. But he didn't come forward because having his name linked with a murder investigation might hurt his chances of obtaining a license to operate a day care center. Besides, he knew nothing about the murder of the Sanibel saleslady other than the fact that it had occurred. For the last time he saw her, Sheila Lankin was alive and well.

Of course, Robert Burton also maintained that the saleswoman was alive the last time *he* saw her. However, the stories of Sheila Lankin's last two walk-ins differed in one significant respect. Burton said that both the victim and the young man were still inside the Egret model when he left Seagull Estates; Dowell claimed they were outside on the front porch. Moreover, Mark stated that they'd walked back to the Pelican model five or ten minutes later, whereupon Sheila went into the office and he got into his car.

When asked if he'd noticed any people or vehicles around when he left the subdivision, Mark mentioned seeing a red truck with white lettering from some landscaping firm. Telling us about the truck was yet another mistake made by the man who thought he could talk his way out of anything.*

Since Mark had nothing more to say about the sequence of events on Wednesday, Wayne asked him if he owned a gun. Dowell said he did, but couldn't remember either the kind or caliber of the gun he'd bought many years ago after his first wife was raped in Ohio. In fact, Mark hadn't laid eyes on the gun since that dreadful episode. It was still packed away in a box in his garage.

Although Wayne had little luck with questions about guns, Ray Rhodes hit the jackpot when he brought in the Bausch and Lomb sunglasses found beside the victim's body. (The glasses had been examined for prints.) Dowell examined them carefully, tried them on and said they were definitely his!

Would Mark be willing to give the SPD the clothes he'd worn on Wednesday? "No problem," replied the remarkably cooperative suspect. Thus, the officers drove Dowell to his home in Cape Coral, where he turned over the clothes and a pair of tan shoes. When asked if he had a pair of gray shoes, Mark assured the policemen that he'd never owned any gray shoes.

Later that afternoon, I asked Robert Burton and Kathy Orwick if they would mind coming to the station to take a look at the clothing and the suspect. Eager to help us solve the crime, they came right over.

After observing Dowell through a two-way mirror, both witnesses positively identified him as the man they had seen on the day of the murder. But they were also positive that he had *not* been wearing any of the clothes we brought over from Cape Coral.

* * *

It didn't take a detective to figure out that Markham William Dowell had given us the wrong clothes, and doubtless a lot of wrong answers as well.

Around six o'clock, a weary yet ever friendly Officer Hinz assured Dowell he was doing his best to eliminate him as a murder suspect.

---

* Dowell's description of the truck enabled us to track down the landscaping firm in question. Our investigation revealed that an employee had been dropped off at the Egret model around 1:30 P.M. on Wednesday, and that man told us he neither saw nor heard anything suspicious while he watered the landscaping around the model home. Therefore, we concluded the murder could not have occurred after 1:30 P.M.

However, Wayne added, it was going to take more time because Dowell seemed to be "a pretty good suspect."

Mark agreed that he appeared to be a pretty good suspect, and the questioning continued. But since Mark was now mad at Ray Rhodes for some reason, Wayne had to carry the ball alone.

"Let's go through this once again," Wayne suggested. And since Dowell didn't mind indulging a dumb cop who was trying so hard to eliminate him as a murder suspect, he repeated everything he'd already revealed. In fact, he even made a new admission: the sales brochure found beside the victim's body was "probably" his.

However, Mark continued to maintain that he and the saleslady were on the front porch of the Egret model when the other walk-in left. The man from Nashville had lied to the police, and Mark wanted to confront him face to face.

Throughout their interview with Dowell, Officers Hinz and Rhodes played entirely different roles. Wayne gave the suspect coffee and cigarettes, but Ray offered him neither tea nor sympathy. Wayne seemed eager to save his neck; Ray seemed eager to wring it.

In view of his bad-guy role, Ray periodically went out of the investigation room in order to leave Mark alone with nice Officer Hinz - and let me know what was going on. When Ray told me that Mark remained adamant about being *outside* the Egret model with Sheila Lankin and had requested a face-to-face meeting with the liar from Nashville, I decided the time had come for me to interview the young man with the Prince Valiant haircut.

*   *   *

Of course, I had to begin the interview by informing the suspect that I was the Chief of the SPD - a revelation guaranteed to put Dowell on the defensive. Therefore, and before asking any questions about the crime, I tried to gain Mark's confidence by expressing considerable concern for both his physical and legal welfare.

Did he want more coffee, cigarettes, or a sandwich? Had Officer Hinz read him his rights? Did he understand his rights? While Dowell assured me Wayne had taken good care of him and he fully understood his rights, I continued to express concern.

"Look Mark," I said, "this is really a very serious matter because you might be charged with murder. But you don't have to talk to me at all. You can call a lawyer right now and ask him to tell you what to do."

Once again, however, Mark remained confident that he could talk his way out of anything without the benefit of legal beagles. For although I was much bigger than Officer Hinz, I appeared to be just as nice - and just as dumb.

Thanks to Dowell's supreme confidence, he answered my questions for nearly an hour. During that time, I concentrated on the sunglasses, gun and clothing, objects the suspect had touched in the Egret model, and his time alone with Sheila Lankin. But since the last answer to a question is often quite different from the first response, I made a point of returning to subjects we had already covered. In several instances, that tactic paid off.

For example, Dowell repeated what he'd already revealed to Officers Hinz and Rhodes: the Bausch and Lomb sunglasses found beside the victim's body were definitely his. When I first asked him how he'd acquired the expensive sunglasses, Mark said someone gave them to him last Christmas. But when I subsequently posed the same question, Dowell admitted that he'd shoplifted the sunglasses from Pearle Vision on Route 41.

"Have you stolen anything else in the Fort Myers area?"

"Just a bottle of Tylenol," he replied.

My questions about the gun seemed to jog Mark's memory. Indeed, he suddenly recalled both the make and caliber of the gun he'd not seen for over five years: a five-shot, .38-caliber Smith and Wesson.

But although we had reason to believe that the person who shot the saleslady was left-handed, I didn't raise that subject while discussing the gun. Instead, I slipped it in when questioning Mark about the jewelry Sheila had worn on Wednesday.

"Are you left-handed?" I inquired out of seemingly idle curiosity.

"Yeah," he said.

When I asked Mark what objects he had touched in the Egret model, he appeared to welcome the opportunity to tell me where we would find his fingerprints. For example, he'd picked up two bars of pink soap because he wanted to smell them. He also had touched the bathroom faucet while getting a drink of water.

"What did you drink out of?" I asked, knowing full well there were no cups in the bathroom.

"I got a drink of water out of my hand," Mark replied, cupping his hand by way of demonstration.

In short, Dowell consistently came up with perfectly reasonable, non-incriminating explanations.

Yet whenever I questioned Mark about the clothes he gave us and the time he spent with Sheila Lankin after the man from Nashville left, he added nothing to what he'd already told Wayne and Ray. The clothes were the ones he wore on Wednesday, and "I've never had any gray shoes." He talked with the saleslady on the front porch of the Egret model, "five minutes, ten minutes at the most," accompanied her back to the office, and said good-bye.

Clearly, I wasn't going to get anything more out of Dowell. So I left the room and called Steve Russell, assistant State's attorney. During my absence, Detective Dick Church continued the interview.

When Mark said he didn't realize he'd left his sunglasses in the model home until he reached for them while driving across the causeway with the sun in his eyes, Detective Church commiserated with him.

"Are your eyes sun-sensitive? Mine are, and the glare really gets to me." But in the midst of a discussion about the glare from the afternoon sun, Dick gave Dowell a jolt.

"How many times did you shoot that woman, Mark?"

"I didn't shoot her at all," he replied as cool as a cucumber.

*   *   *

Unfortunately, I didn't have any better luck with Steve Russell than Detective Church had with Dowell. For when I reported the results of our investigation, Steve told me we didn't have a case - and urged me not to arrest the suspect on such circumstantial evidence.

Of course, all lawyers like open-and-shut cases they can win in court. Winning enhances a lawyer's reputation, and fees. However, a State's attorney falls into a different category, for his job is to ensure that the court's time and the taxpayers' money are not wasted on cases the State can't win. As a result, a State's attorney is a very powerful and extremely cautious person.

After talking with Steve Russell, I turned to Ray Rhodes and let off a bit of steam. "I don't give a shit what the State's attorney says. There's no way this son of a bitch is getting out of here without being arrested!"

Once again, a damn-the-torpedoes decision had a calming effect. I returned to the investigation room and told Dowell I was about to arrest him for Murder One and Robbery.

"So if there's anything else you want to tell me, Mark, now's the time to do it. Because once I arrest you and your lawyer arrives, the talking is over."

Mark replied that he had nothing to add to what he'd already said, and I placed him under arrest at 7:23 P.M. Following that formality, I again asked Dowell if he wanted to call a lawyer. He did not. However, he'd like to continue discussing this matter with us, and have a "group session" with Robert Burton and Kathy Orwick!

But when Mark realized that we weren't the least bit interested in either a group session or a suspect who had nothing more to say, he finally called a lawyer and attorney Taminosian arrived at the station around ten-thirty. Shortly thereafter, nice Officer Hinz drove Dowell to Friendly Frank's Hotel, a.k.a. the Lee County Jail.

* * *

With Dowell safely behind bars, Sanibelians breathed a sigh of relief - and heaped praise upon the SPD. In their eyes, the case was closed. But in my eyes, it was wide open because Steve Russell was absolutely right: no jury would convict our prime suspect on the basis of circumstantial evidence.

Therefore, the SPD had to produce more compelling proof to persuade a jury "beyond a reasonable doubt" that Markham William Dowell was guilty as charged. Not surprisingly, the investigation continued for several months. But although we had no way of knowing it at the time, our big break came just a few hours before I arrested Mark.

Soon after Wayne and Ray Rhodes left Dowell's home in Cape Coral, Officer Lew Phillips arrived with a search warrant and several deputies from the Lee County Sheriff's Department. Upon entering the residence, one of the deputies remarked that it looked like a model home. Indeed the house was filled to the gills with fancy furniture, designer rugs, expensive paintings, plug-in appliances, soft towels, and scented soaps.

Yet since the search warrant had nothing to do with home decor, but everything to do with a .38-caliber gun and ammunition, the policemen concentrated on the latter. Although they failed to find the gun, they discovered a real bonanza on a closet shelf: a box containing five, .38-caliber Winchester bullets - identical to those removed from Sheila Lankin's body.

Of course, what appears to be identical may not prove to be identical. But thanks to Steve Russell, I learned that the FBI had developed a process for comparing bullet lead. Therefore, we sent both sets of bullets to the FBI for analysis and, in late March of '85, received a report stating that they came from the same lead batch. However, and greatly to his credit, Russell flew to Washington, D.C. for further clarification.

The FBI's analyst explained that the chances of having two *different* sets of bullets from the same lead batch end up in Fort Myers at the same time were extremely remote. Backed by the expert's opinion, the Assistant State Attorney was now prepared to argue that, "the likelihood that Markham Dowell would just by happenstance possess that same type of ammunition manufactured from the same source and at or about the same time as some other person who possessed like bullets fired through the body of Sheila Lankin was virtually impossible."

In the meantime, the SPD was busy building its case, a tedious step-by-step procedure one rarely sees in movies or on TV. For catching a killer is exciting, but gathering evidence is generally boring. Boring or not, however, it's an essential part of police work - and invariably involves patience, perseverance, and piles of paperwork.

In addition to checking out the alibis of Kornbluth, Wojciechowski, Ron Levy and Jerry Lankin, we contacted the police in Tennessee with regard to Robert Lipscomb Burton, Jr. Fortunately, our star witness turned out to be squeaky clean: no criminal record, no warrants, not even a traffic violation.

However, I was far less satisfied with the results of the SPD's background investigation of the young Dowells. For despite full cooperation from our fellow officers in five states where either Vicky or Mark had lived, we learned very little.

Mark's driver's license had been suspended a few times, and he owed some $800 in fines. No big deal in a country where thousands of people drive around on suspended licenses and never dream of committing murder or armed robbery in order to pay their fine to the Department of Motor Vehicles.

Moreover, Vicky Dowell appeared to be cleaner than Caesar's wife. But when we ran another check under her *maiden* name, we found that Vicky Gay Pitvorec was wanted for Grand Theft in Orlando, Florida. However, we learned considerably more about the Dowells from Vicky's sister and brother-in-law, Mary and Tom Kolar of Fort Myers Beach. For there's no honor among thieves, and blood is thinner than water when relatives are out to save their own skins.

* * *

According to Tom Kolar, the Dowells occupied themselves in a rather unconventional manner after arriving in the Fort Myers area some eighteen months ago. Specifically, the young couple spent a great deal of their time visiting model homes during the day and burglarizing them at night. And since the Kolars had been deeply involved in this illicit activity, Tom (upon his father's insistence and his lawyer's advice), decided that it was now his duty to rat on his relatives.*

Tom told us that he and Mary frequently accompanied the Dowells on their visits to model homes, presenting themselves as prospective buyers. While the others distracted the salesperson

---

* When Kolar's father heard that Mark had been arrested for murder, he helped Tom get rid of his loot. Together, father and son dropped stolen goods into dumpsters throughout Fort Myers Beach.

with questions, one "prospective buyer" wandered off and unlocked a door or window. Later, under cover of darkness, the walk-ins returned to the model home and walked out with whatever they wanted.

As I listened to tattletale Tom, I realized that he was very impressed by Mark's ability to bombard salespersons with questions about local schools, hardwood floors, jacuzzis and other amenities. However, Kolar was even more impressed by the fact that Dowell had burglarized twenty-three model homes and had never been caught! For although Tom had not participated in all those burglaries, he'd been involved long enough to know that Mark could talk his way out of anything.

As proof, Kolar cited several close calls. For example, Mark managed to convince the deputy sheriff who stopped them with a trailer full of stolen furniture that they were delivering it rather than stealing it.

Although Kolar contributed little to the SPD's murder investigation, we immediately contacted law-enforcement agencies in the Fort Myers area in connection with their model-home burglaries. As a result, the police in Cape Coral obtained a search warrant and found over sixty stolen items in the Dowell residence.

"The preponderance of the items present in the residence being such that would establish knowledge on the part of the occupants that the property was stolen," said CCPD's Detective Nicholl, who placed Vicky under arrest for Grand Theft. Thus, one month after Mark's arrest, Vicky Gay Pitvorec Dowell joined her husband at the Lee County Jail - separate cells, of course.

Not surprisingly, Vicky didn't like Friendly Frank's Hotel at all. Therefore, and in order to avoid spending time behind bars for burglary, she turned state's evidence and testified against her husband during his trial for murder. Specifically, Vicky told the court that when the Dowells (with "terrible two" in tow) drove from Cape Coral to the SPD on Friday, January 11, Mark made a slight detour and dropped his gray shoes into a dumpster.*

---

* Contrary to popular belief, a wife can testify against her husband (and vice versa), for the husband-wife "privilege" applies only to confidential communications. Thus, Vicky couldn't tell the jury anything her husband said to her, but she could tell them what she had seen him do.

Throughout his trial, the man with a gift for gab didn't say a word. For the two lawyers who represented him had finally succeeded in persuading Dowell that his only chance of avoiding a date with the electric chair lay in keeping his mouth shut.

But although the prosecuting attorney had no opportunity to make mincemeat out of Mark on the witness stand, Steve Russell managed to convince the jury that the defendant was indeed guilty as charged. Subsequently, Judge Thomas Reese informed Markham William Dowell that "It is the sentence of this court that you are committed to the Department of Corrections for your natural life."

Yet while satisfied with the jury's verdict and the judge's sentence, I had a frustrating feeling that Dowell would *not* be spending the rest of his life behind bars. For a judge's sentence generally bears little relation to actual time served, especially in a state where the problem of overcrowded prisons has reached monumental proportions. Florida "solves" that problem by releasing those who committed past crimes in order to make room for those who have committed more recent crimes.

SANIBEL POLICE DEPARTMENT
P.O. Box 438
SANIBEL, FLORIDA 33957

Phone: (813) 472-3111
IN CUSTODY-   MURDER AND ROBBERY OF REAL ESTATE SALES LADY

DESCRIPTION: Markham William Dowell
w/m 29 years, D.O.B. 1/20/55, 5'11"
195 lbs., blue eyes, light brown hair
Well groomed, wears designer clothes,
speaks with good English and intelli-
gently.   Has worked as a Food and
Beverage Manager in Louisville, Kentucky
and St. Louis, Missouri.

ALIAS: Mark Boselo and Bill Ellis

WEAPON: Subject's known to have in
his possession a blued Charter Arm
revolver, undercover model, 38 caliber
Ser. #546-436.

VEHICLE: 1981 light to medium green
Model 4000 Audi Vin WAUDD0816DC103264
registered in Kentucky from 9/1/82 to
7/31/83, Kentucky license FMN814;
presently registered in Missouri,
license SZM 668
SSN 275-42-3540

ARRESTED: BURGLARY

DESCRIPTION: Vicky Gay (Pitvorec)
Dowell, w/f, D.O.B. 12/25/56, 5'8"
119 lbs. green eyes, brown hair
SS No. 365-66-4335

SANIBEL POLICE DEPARTMENT   - SANIBEL, FLORIDA

GENERAL INFORMATION - MURDER AND ROBBERY

MARKHAM WILLIAM DOWELL was arrested January 11, 1985 by the
Sanibel, Florida, Police Department for MURDER AND ROBBERY.
The murder occurred January 9, 1985 between 1:00 and 1:30 p.m.
in a model home on Sanibel. The victim was shot twice in the
back at close range. The victim was also struck on the back
of the head by an unknown object.

A ring, described as a wide gold band with approximately 3 karat
heart-shaped diamond, along with a gold serpentine chain with a
penny-sized Sagitarrius sign of the Zodiac were taken from the
victim. The weapon used in this homicide and the jewelry have
not been recovered.

The victim had been showing model homes through the day and Mark
Dowell was the last person to be seen with her.

GENERAL INFORMATION - MODEL HOME BURGLARY

MARKHAM WILLIAM DOWELL and wife, VICKY GAY DOWELL, went to
numerous model homes in the Fort Myers, Cape Coral, Sanibel,
Lee County area as prospective buyers in the day time. Mark
Dowell is known to have talked to real estate persons where he
would state that he was looking for a two story house; asking
about jacuzzis; asking about wooden floors being included in
the price of the home; said he had two children and was concerned
with the school districts. When by himself, he would remark
that his wife was in another city looking at real estate as he
was planning on moving into the area. Dowell, with his wife Vicky,
and at times with his brother-in-law and sister-in-law, Tom and
Mary Kolar, would enter model homes as prospective buyers, and
while keeping the sales person occupied, one person would unlock
a door or window. These people would then return at night and
burglarize the model home, taking furniture, throw rugs, pictures,
towels, soap and other items.

SANIBEL POLICE DEPARTMENT IS REQUESTING ANY PERSON WHO HAS HAD
CONTACT WITH MARK OR VICKY DOWELL OR HAS KNOWLEDGE OF SIMILAR
TYPE OF CRIMES, TO CALL COLLECT, THE SANIBEL POLICE DEPARTMENT
813-472-3111.

page two

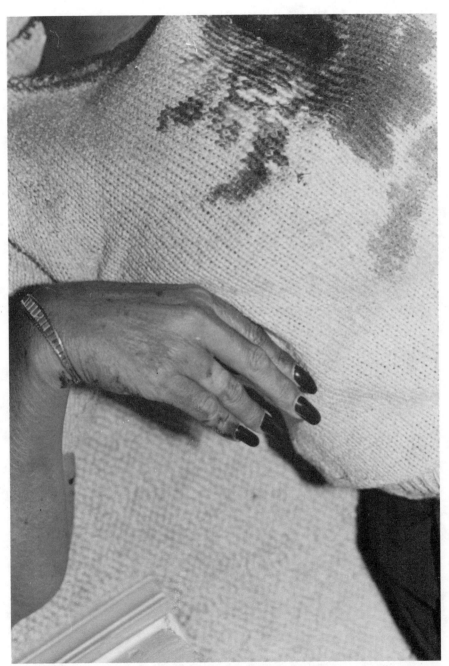

A sharp-eyed medical examiner noticed a band of white skin on Sheila's ring finger.

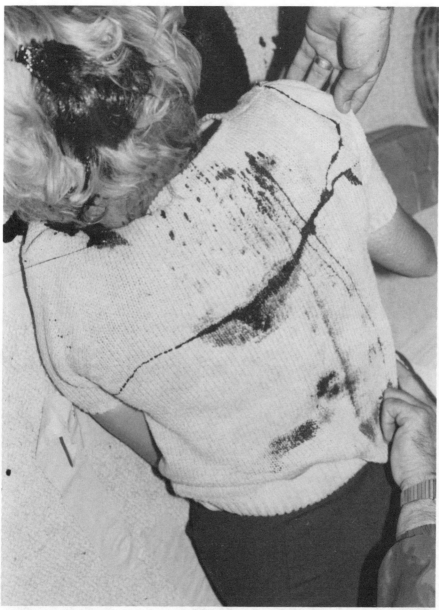

Blood droppings on the back of her sweater, dining room table, and hall-way indicate she was struck on the head in the dining room and forced into the master bed and bathrooms, before being shot twice in the back. Bullet entrance wounds denoted by gunpowder burns on the back of her sweater.

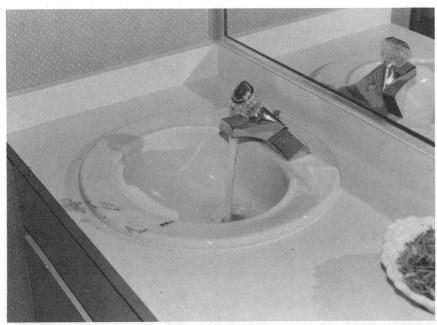

Blood on the mirror, counter, sink and faucet. (Still running) no drinking glass or cup.

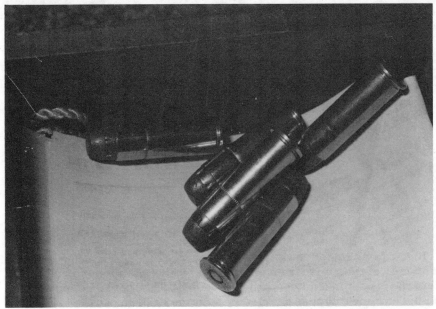

Box containing five .38 caliber bullets. Discovered at Dowell's home.

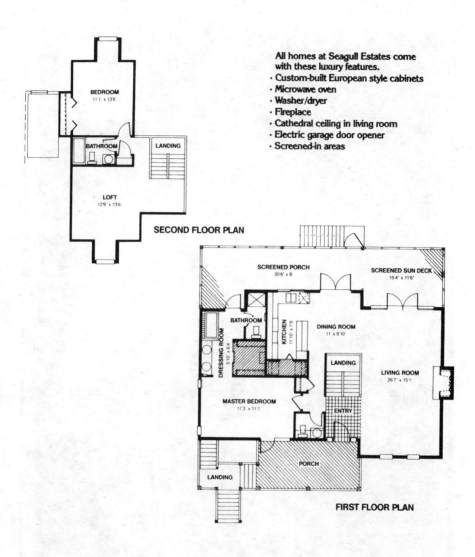

BEDROOM
11'1" x 13'6"

BATHROOM

LANDING

LOFT
12'9" x 13'6"

SECOND FLOOR PLAN

All homes at Seagull Estates come
with these luxury features.
· Custom-built European style cabinets
· Microwave oven
· Washer/dryer
· Fireplace
· Cathedral ceiling in living room
· Electric garage door opener
· Screened-in areas

SCREENED PORCH
30'8" x 8'

SCREENED SUN DECK
15'4" x 11'6"

BATHROOM

KITCHEN
11'10" x 7'9"

DINING ROOM
11' x 9'10"

DRESSING ROOM
5'10" x 6'4"

LANDING

LIVING ROOM
26'7" x 15'1"

MASTER BEDROOM
17'3" x 11'1"

ENTRY

PORCH

LANDING

FIRST FLOOR PLAN

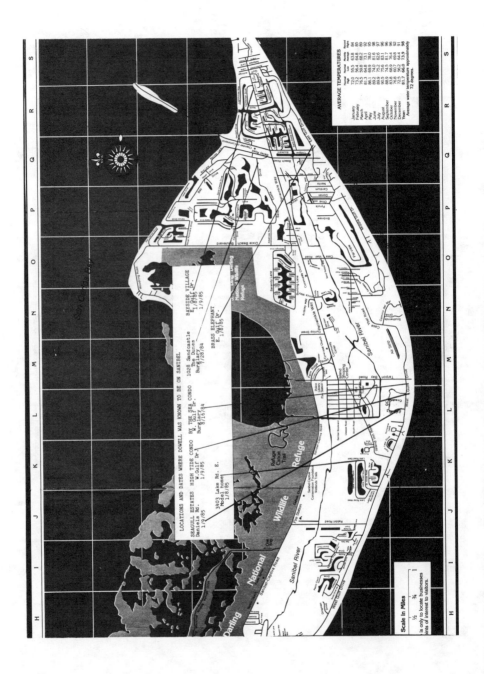

THE BEGINNING
OF THE END

During my twelve-and-a-half years as Chief of the SPD, Sanibel was tranformed into a full-fledged resort. Indeed, the small barrier island soon received well over one million visitors a year, and property values soared to over one billion dollars. Since criminals found such statistics extremely appealing, crime prevention was always a top priority for the SPD.

Therefore, I was both confused and frustrated by the fact that the people who ran city hall never asked the police to do a routine background check on anyone they proposed to hire - not even the highly paid, highly powerful, city managers! Thus, from time to time, I had to deal with complaints about city employees who, for one reason or another, should never have been hired. Chief among them was a convicted felon with an impressive rap sheet.

Donald Irvin Howze's criminal career included a series of arrests for carrying concealed weapons, firing guns within city limits, resisting arrest with violence, and aggravated assault. Convicted of beating up a Florida policeman, Howze spent five years in prison.

Soon after the ex-con's release from Raiford in 1983, he was hired by Gary Price, then-Director of the Public Works Department and Assistant City Manager.

* * *

Friday October 14

After drinking vodka all day, Donald Howze went to his sister's home in the Periwinkle Trailer Park. Mildred was not at all happy to see him. She became even less happy when her brother decided to beat up her boyfriend. Thus, around 6:15 P.M., the SPD dispatcher received a "disturbance call" from Mildred Howze, Sanibel's Clerk/Treasurer.

When Officer Don Case arrived at the scene, he found a small, orderly group standing outside the modest home on Lot 110. Among them were brothers Dick and Jerry Muench (Jerry was then a planning commissioner), a mortified Mildred, her boyfriend from Lot 104, a deputy from the Lee County Sheriff's Department, and SPD Officer Scott Ashby. The only disorderly person on the premises was Donald Howze - supine, and shouting a steady stream of obscenities.

Following a brief discussion with Mildred, the complainant, Officer Case asked Donald to stand up - a simple exercise the latter proved incapable of performing without assistance from both SPD officers. Once the wobbling Howze was in a relatively upright position, Officer Case placed him under arrest for disorderly intoxication.

Unfortunately, Donald took an extraordinarily dim view of that pronouncement and the handcuffs placed on his wrists. He threatened to shoot Scott Ashby ("I'm gonna catch you off duty and blow your motherfucking ass away!"), and also threatened to kill Don Case, the Muench brothers, and me.

Not surprisingly, our officers encountered "considerable difficulty putting Howze in the rear of the cruiser." Specifically they tried to shove him in without bruising his besotted body, thereby laying themselves open to the charge of police brutality. Doubtless aware of their dilemma, Donald took full advantage of it. He kicked Officer Case in the face, and kicked Officer Ashby's hand - jamming his thumb.

Far too violent to sit still for a photo-and-fingerprint session at the station, Howze was transported directly to the Lee County Jail. Realizing that Donald was not a happy camper, the personnel at Friendly Frank's Hotel decided not to take his picture and prints until he calmed down. But since Donald Irvin Howze had threatened to

shoot five people, the SPD needed to know more about him sooner
rather than later. Therefore, Don Case called Mildred.

According to Mildred, her brother didn't own a gun. He did, however, have a severe drinking problem and became extremely violent
when drunk. And, much to Mildred's embarrassment, Donald also
had a police record and had spent time in prison.

Armed with this information, Don Case tried to obtain a criminal
history by teletype. But, since communications were down, the SPD
didn't receive the full report of Donald's criminal career until late
the following afternoon. By that time, Howze was already out on
bail.

Saturday October 15

Around 11:00 P.M., a weary Officer Ashby left the SPD and
headed for his car. On his way down to the parking area under the
station in the new city hall, Scott passed Officer Leanos. "You be
careful, Art," he warned the Greek-American coming on duty. But
the armed individual hiding in the dark wasn't waiting for Art. He
was waiting for the light to go on when Scott opened his car door -
and became an illuminated target.

Right after Ashby opened the door, he heard a loud gunshot and
what sounded like a bullet striking the concrete column behind him.
Diving onto the front seat of his car for cover, Scott's first coherent
thought was that the ex-con who had threatened to blow him away
yesterday was carrying out the threat today. "Get down! Somebody's shooting at us!" he shouted to Leanos, who had rushed over to
see what was going on.

Ashby and Leanos were not the only policemen who heard the
gunshot. In the SPD office upstairs, Officers Case and Blackmore
also heard a loud shot coming from the parking area beneath the
building. Both men ran down to the parking area, where the embat-
tled Scott and Art reported that someone was shooting at them. Officer Case immediately took charge of the situation.

A long-time resident and former proprietor of the highly popular
Harbor House Restaurant (which received a rave review from the
New York *Times*), Citizen Case would doubtless have found it hard
to believe that such an incident could occur on Sanibel. But Officer
Case didn't find it all hard to believe. For just a few years ago, a de-

mented Don Hiers had held him hostage at gunpoint. And, just one day ago, a drunken Donald Howze had threatened to blow his brains out. Therefore, Case took the matter seriously, and pursued it in a thoroughly professional manner.

Specifically, Case had Ashby and Leanos cruise the area west of city hall, while he cruised the area east of said expensive, award-winning edifice. But the cruisers' spotlights failed to flush anyone out of the bushes, or illuminate any vehicles or pedestrians.

Alerted by the dispatcher, I arrived at the station with Officers Applegate and Molnar shortly after the cruisers returned. Well-armed and as protected as possible, our men searched the entire city-hall complex.

When we failed to find anyone, we decided to look for the most likely suspect: Donald Howze. For by this time, the SPD knew that the man who had threatened to kill Case, Ashby, *et al.* the previous evening was a convicted felon, violent when drunk, and no longer a guest at Friendly Frank's Hotel. Thus, as Case concluded in his report, "There seemed to be a good possibility that this subject could have been responsible for the shot." But if so, where was he?

Don Case had good reason to believe the suspect might be hiding out in Doug Quimby's apartment. Indeed, Don told me he had several good reasons for reaching that conclusion. Both Quimby and Howze worked in the same department (Public Works), and were thought to be friends. Moreover, Doug's apartment on Palm Ridge Road was within walking distance of city hall and, in all likelihood, currently unoccupied. For since Douglas Quimby had married Rose that very day, the newlyweds were probably off on their honeymoon.

We also had reason to believe the suspect might have gone to the residence of Sue Baird, a former city employee who lived off Periwinkle Way in an area realtors refer to as "centrally located" - i.e., run-down but affordable. Sue and Donald Howze were known to be close friends, and had been seen together earlier that evening.

Thus, after directing Officers Ashby and Molnar to check out the nearby Quimby apartment, Don Case accompanied me to Sue Baird's residence off Periwinkle. Of course, Scott and Jeff reached their destination before Don and I reached ours. However, we all approached the respective residences with drawn weapons - standard operating procedure (SOP) when attempting to apprehend or locate an armed suspect.

Sunday October 16

Scott and Jeff arrived at Quimby's home around 12:05 A.M., and immediately became suspicious when they saw lights on and heard sounds coming from the apartment of newlyweds presumed to be off on their honeymoon. After knocking on the door, and receiving no response, the officers went to the landlord's apartment and explained the reason for their presence. In view of the unusual circumstances the landlord gave them the key to Quimby's apartment - and his permission to enter it.

Ashby and Molnar returned to Quimby's apartment and, once again, knocked on the door. Still no response. They unlocked the door, entered, and saw Doug Quimby sprawled on the couch watching a loud TV show. "Are you all right, Doug? Are you alone?" Jeff asked.

Receiving no reply from the bewildered bridegroom, Jeff repeated his questions - at which point the bride emerged from the bathroom. "Is everything all right?" Scott asked the equally bewildered bride. But Rose quickly recovered from her confusion.

"What's going on?" she asked. "Is this some kind of joke?" Since Rose knew that her husband and Jeff Molnar were good buddies, such a joke was not beyond the realm of possibility.

Jeff immediately assured the Quimbys that it wasn't a bad joke, and told them about Howze's threats and the shooting incident at city hall. Jeff also explained why he and Scott became suspicious when they saw lights on in the apartment, and apologized for any inconvenience they may have caused. Far from being upset, the Quimbys expressed appreciation for the SPD's concern and alertness.

* * *

Like the Quimbys, Sue Baird didn't appear to be either upset or annoyed when Don Case and I arrived at her home with drawn weapons. And despite the fact that it was after midnight, she didn't tell us to go fly a kite and come back at a more civilized hour. Instead, Sue assured us that she and Howze had been together for

four hours on the evening of the shooting incident, and launched into a recital of their activities - all of which allegedly took place off-island.

According to Ms. Baird's watch, the date with Donald began when
she arrived at his trailer in the Siesta Bay Recreational Park on
Summerlin Road at 7:15 P.M. Although Sue spent nearly two hours
in the trailer, the woman in her fifties said nothing about what went
on there between her and the ex-con in his forties. But whatever
happened must have made them hungry. As a result, Sue drove
Donald to the Prawnbroker Restaurant in Fort Myers around 9:00
P.M.

They both ordered seafood platters, the bill came to $28.25,
Donald paid with two, twenty-dollar bills, and received $11.75 in
change. Sue said nothing about a tip. However, she did describe
Donald's attire in minute detail - including every snap-down button
on his western shirt.

When Sue glanced at her watch and realized it was eleven o'clock,
the couple left the restaurant. Sue dropped Donald off at his trailer
around 11:10 P.M., and returned to her Sanibel home at precisely
11:30. How did Ms. Baird know the precise time? She looked at her
watch while opening the door because she heard the phone ringing.

Instead of allaying my suspicions, Sue Baird's description of her
date with Donald ran up a red flag. For in my experience, few people
can recall so many details, and even fewer consult their watches at
the times a court of law would consider crucial.

Since I had no reason to believe that Ms. Baird was an extraordinarily rare individual blessed with *both* total recall and an uncanny
propensity to consult her watch at critical times, I suspected her
statements might well be designed to establish an alibi rather than
reveal the truth.

Doubtless sensing my skepticism, Sue readily agreed to show us
where Donald lived. I immediately contacted Officers Ashby and
Molnar and told them to follow us across the causeway to Siesta Bay
Recreational Park. When we arrived, a light was on in Howze's trailer and his pickup was parked in the driveway.

Since the roads were wet from rain, I checked the truck's tires.
They were dry. Clearly, Howze had not driven his pickup for several

hours. However, he could have used some other vehicle. If so, the suspect might still be at large. On the other hand, he might well be at home and in bed.

Seeing no movement inside the lighted trailer, I decided not to knock on the door to determine whether Donald was indeed at home. After all, Ms. Baird had given him a good alibi, it was now nearly one o'clock in the morning, and the chances of persuading the ex-con to open his door and talk to the police at any time were nil. We would only get into a pissing match. Besides, we had no physical evidence to place Howze at the scene, and no one had seen him in the general vicinity.

It is always best to have armed subjects outside in the open. Therefore, I told Scott and Jeff to watch Howze's trailer, and to stop him if he appeared - in which case we would go over the situation with him. But since there was no movement for the next several hours we cancelled the detail.

Monday October 17
In the morning, it was business as usual. Donald Howze reported for work and was out mowing the lawn around city hall. The Assistant City Manager, Gary Price, came to my office and asked how the hell Commissioner Jerry Muench knew about Howze's criminal record.

I told Gary that I really didn't know how Muench found out about Donald's record. But since Jerry had come to the station following Howze's arrest, I suggested that he might have seen the record on an officer's desk - or an officer might have mentioned it to him. Interestingly enough, Gary Price never asked about either the incident at the trailer park or the alleged shooting at city hall.

In any event, I saw no point in questioning the man who was cutting the grass as I knew he'd learned one thing (if nothing else) in prison: his right to refuse to talk to the police. Also, the assistant city manager's attitude didn't help the situation.

Around 3:00 P.M., I received a formal memorandum from then-City Manager Bernard J. Murphy, Jr.

"It has just been brought to my attention" he began (but didn't say by whom), that two officers made an "unauthorized entry" into Douglas Quimby's apartment "with drawn weapons." The C.M. ex-

pressed "very serious concerns" about such activity, and ordered me
to provide him with a full explanation and all pertinent information
by 4:00 P.M. the following day. Since Bernie was my boss, I took his
very serious concerns very seriously.

Not surprisingly, many Sanibelians believe their elected officials
run city hall. In fact, and with the sole exception of the legal department, the non-elected city manager is in charge of all departments
- including the SPD.

Therefore, Bernie could have obtained any information he wanted
simply by picking up the phone, or strolling down to my office. However, since he elected to write a formal memorandum, I had no
choice but to treat it as a formal complaint. Specifically, No. 5345-
83: Complaint Against Officers.

While the city manager knew little about law enforcement, he
knew even less about the rights of Florida's law-enforcement officers, the rights of Sanibel's employees (including members of the
SPD), or SOP when seeking suspects thought to be armed and dangerous. Thus, in dealing with Complaint No. 5345-83, I tried to sat-
isfy the demands of the city manager's memorandum without de-
priving my officers of their rights.

Sanibel's Personnel Management System states that a Department Director must inform an employee of any complaint, provide a
copy of the complaint (if written), and give the employee three days
to respond in writing. Moreover, State Statue 112.532 specifies that
a law-enforcement officer has the right to know the names of all
complainants. But Bernie Murphy's memorandum set a twenty-
four-hour deadline, and didn't reveal the name of the person who
originated the Complaint Against Officers.

Therefore, I provided Officers Ashby and Molnar with a copy of
the memorandum, and gave them three days to prepare Supplemen-
tary Offense Reports - the time-consuming "supps" that are the
bane of all policemen, especially hunt-and-peck typists. I also
assured Scott and Jeff that we would interview Doug Quimby to determine whether he had initiated the complaint against them. In
fact, and some forty minutes after I received the problematical
memorandum, Officer Lew Phillips interviewed the alleged victim
of unauthorized entry with drawn weapons.

During the interview, Quimby stated that he had not complained about the officers, and didn't want to press any charges against them. Both he and his wife appreciated the SPD's concern, and had not felt threatened by the weapons that the officers pointed toward the ceiling. But although Doug Quimby wasn't a complainant, I noted that his signed statement contained the names of two people who *might* have originated the Complaint Against Officers. One was Quimby's supervisor in the Public Works Department, Steve Morton.

When Lew interviewed Quimby, the latter made it perfectly clear that he and Howze were not friends by any stretch of the imagination. Indeed, Doug considered the ex-con "unpredictable," and was often afraid of him because "he is quick tempered and you don't know what he's going to do." Thus, after learning about Howze's threats and possible involvement in the shooting incident, Doug called his supervisor early Sunday morning.

"Did they put Don in jail?" he asked the sleepy Steve Morton. But when the supervisor said he didn't know what the bridegroom was talking about, Doug filled him in on the details - including the appearance of two SPD officers at his apartment shortly after midnight.

However, the purpose of Quimby's call was not to lodge a complaint against the police. Rather, it was to inform his supervisor that, should Howze come to work on Monday, he "didn't want to be around the guy."

Therefore, I considered the other person named in Quimby's statement, Gary Price, the more likely complainant. For I had recently been obliged to bring two complaints to Gary's attention, which undoubtedly caused him to take an exceedingly dim view of the SPD.

* * *

The first problem concerned a city employee who wanted to leave Price's Public Works Department and join the SPD. But while taking a lie-detector test, the applicant admitted to using cocaine. Thus, there was no way I could avoid bringing the employee's drug use to Gary's attention. Although I sensed that Price didn't want to hear about it - and wasn't inclined to do anything about it - I'd done my duty by reporting it.

Unfortunately, the other complaint proved to be far more problematical. For the complainant in question was Gary's second wife, who was in the process of divorcing him. According to Mrs. Price, her employer (Sanibel's Postmaster) had told her to go to the SPD and ask us to put a stop to her husband's unauthorized entries into the area strictly reserved for postal employees.

Moreover, Mrs. Price complained that in addition to harassing her at work, her estranged husband frequently threatened her while she was on her mail route. Hence, I had the dubious pleasure of informing Gary of his wife's formal complaint and discussing it with him. Although Gary stopped threatening and harassing his wife, he now had a real scunner against the SPD.

As a result, I wasn't at all surprised to learn that, according to Doug Quimby, Gary Price had contacted him *before* his interview with Lew Phillips and told him that "some heads are going to roll in the SPD." But since Officer Phillips was a thoroughly professional policeman, he tactfully refrained from referring to rolling heads. Instead he reported that the assistant city manager indicated to the alleged victim that "there would be some action taken in the matter."

Yet despite the fact that my men had the right to know who had initiated the complaint, I couldn't provide that information. All I could tell them was that it might have been Gary Price.

Tuesday October 18

First thing in the morning, I responded to the city manager's one-page memorandum with a three-page memorandum. It contained pertinent quotations from state statutes and Sanibel's Personnel Management System, clarifications of the preceding, and an explanation of standard operating procedure when dealing with armed suspects. Should Bernie consider the SOP "improper," I suggested that he advise me of his "recommendations for a procedure to handle this type of situation."

My memorandum also listed several enclosures for the city manager's review. Chief among them were Complaint No. 5345-83,

Quimby's statement, police reports of the shooting incident, and detailed "supps" from Officers Ashby and Molnar (who must have burned the midnight oil to help me meet the C.M.'s twenty-four-hour deadline). I concluded that "no further investigation is warranted in this matter," and indicated that I was sending a copy of my memorandum to the city attorney as required by Sanibel's Personnel Management System.

Having met the city manager's demand for a full explanation, the ball was now in Bernie's court and I waited for his response. I didn't have long to wait.

Apoplectic with rage, Bernard J. Murphy, Jr., fired off a two-page memorandum and sent copies to Officers Case, Blackmore, Ashby and Molnar, Mr. and Mrs. Quimby, the city attorney, and the man who would be in complete charge while Bernie was on vacation - Acting City Manager Gary A. Price.

While the city manager knew nothing about police work, he was a superb tactician who knew that the best defense is a strong offense. Therefore, he didn't question the rights of Sanibel's police officers or standard operating procedure. Instead he expressed "extreme disappoinment" in my failure to understand his memorandum of October 17. Had I read it "more carefully," I would certainly have realized that Bernie was merely asking me to provide "a report about the matter that may have been innocuous, but may also have been very serious."

Unfortunately, the city manager didn't explain how I could provide such a report without gathering all the facts and conducting an investigation. "Please be advised," Bernie wrote, that future requests for a full report and explanation should not be construed as either a complaint or an investigation. Rather, he concluded, "I would hope you would put these inquiries into perspective."

Of course, the city manager had both the right and the responsibility to be fully informed about what went on in the departments under his jurisdiction. Therefore, I had made a point of sending him a copy of every SPD report he might conceivably be interested in seeing, such as the arrest of employee Howze on Friday and the shooting incident at city hall on Saturday. Neither of the preceding elicited any inquiries from the city manager or any member of the council.

But when Bernie formally expressed serious concerns about drawn weapons in general and unauthorized entry in particular, there was no way I could put those inquiries into perspective. For an officer who makes an unauthorized entry into a person's home has committed a federal offense, and may be sentenced to spend time in a federal prison.

Although Bernie Murphy's second memorandum criticized my own performance, it also let my men off the hook. "I have a great deal of confidence in Officer Molnar and Officer Ashby" and, he added, no intention of lodging a formal complaint or launching an investigation.

However, the city manager's final sentence clearly indicated that I would not be one of the beneficiaries of his second thoughts: "We will discuss the matter more fully when I return."

Friday October 28

Ten days later, while Bernie Murphy was on vacation, an anxious Mildred Howze contacted the SPD. Mildred reported that her brother was extremely despondent, and she feared he might kill her, her boyfriend, and himself. I knew only too well that, drunk or sober, Donald was indeed a dangerous man.

Therefore, I provided Mildred with a hand-held police radio for her home in the trailer park, and directed all SPD personnel to take special precautionary measures to protect themselves and city hall. I also explained the situation and the steps taken to deal with it in a memorandum to Acting City Manager Gary Price.

Shortly thereafter, the ex-con was terminated from the Public Works Department. Moreover, and much to the relief of Mildred Howze and all members of the SPD, Donald drifted away. Bernie Murphy returned from his vacation both refreshed and better able to put the realities of police work into perspective. As a result, we never did get around to discussing the matter more fully.

Despite our brief battle of the memoranda, the city manager and I continued to enjoy an excellent professional relationship and remained on friendly terms. Thus, like most islanders and city hall employees, I was extremely sorry when Bernie Murphy resigned the following year to become city manager somewhere in Massachusetts. But before he left, Bernie made a point of stopping by the station, something few politicians challenged by a subordinate would ever dream of doing. "I just wanted to tell you," he said, "that this is the finest police department I've ever worked with - and you're the best police chief I've ever known."

Basking in the generous praise bestowed by my former boss, I wished him well in wintry New England.

MEMORANDUM

DATE: October 17, 1983

TO: Police Chief

FROM: City Manager

It has just been brought to my attention that members of our department made an unauthorized entry into the apartment of Douglas Quimby, 2420 Palm Ridge Road, sometime Saturday evening, October 15, 1983. I also understand that this alleged entry was made in connection with the alleged shooting incident on City Hall property.

It is further my understanding that they obtained a key from someone and entered the apartment with drawn weapons, only to find Mr. and Mrs. Quimby retired for the evening.

If this information is correct, I have very serious concerns about such activity. Please provide me with an explanation and information by Tuesday, October 18 at 4:00 P.M.

Bernard J. Murphy, Jr.,
City Manager

BJM:VJS

October 18, 1983

TO: City Manager Murphy
  cc:City Attorney LaCroix

FROM: Chief Butler

RE: (1) Your memorandum dated October 17, 1983 and received by
         my office at 3:00 p.m., October 17, 1983.

     (2) Sanibel Police Department reports:
         5307-83   5:46 p.m.   10/14/83   Arrest of City Employee
         5321-83   11:00 p.m.   10/15/83   Shots fired at Sanibel
                                             Police
     (3) State Statue 112.533 - Receipt and processing of complaints
                                 against police officers.

     (4) State Statute 112.532 - Law Enforcement Officers Bill of Rights

     (5) City of Sanibel PERSONNEL MANAGEMENT SYSTEM 17.8 - Complaints
         and investigations.

     (6) Sanibel Police Department, RULES, REGULATIONS AND POLICY

Please be advised of the following:

1. Complaint and Investigation 17.8 (A) CITY OF SANIBEL PERSONNEL
   MANAGEMENT SYSTEM adopted by Resolution 83-40, September 20, 1983.

A copy of your memo was given to Police Officers Ashby and Molnar and
they were advised they had three days to repond in writing to the
alleged complaint.

2. LAW ENFORCEMENT OFFICERS RIGHTS - State Statute 112.532.

This chapter was complied with. Under section (d) "The law
enforcement officer under investigation shall be informed of the nature
of the investigation prior to any interrogation, and he shall be
informed of the name of all complainants.", the Police Officers
were advised that Douglas Quimby, the alleged victim, would be
interviewed to ascertain who originated the complaint.

A sworn statement was then taken from George Douglas Quimby, an
employee of the City of Sanibel and residing at 2420 Palm Ridge
Road, Sanibel, Fl. at 3:38 p.m., October 17, 1983.

Mr. Quimby, in his statement, stated that he did not make any
complaints against Officers Ashby and Molnar, but that he had informed his supervisor, Steve Morton, early Sunday morning and
asked him if Don Howze had been taken to jail. His supervisor
asked why and he told his supervisor what had taken place at
his home when the police arrived. He further stated the reason he
had made inquiry to his supervisor was that he didn't want to be
around Don Howze. Mr. Quimby stated that prior to giving the
statement to our department, he had been notified by Assistant
City Manager Gary Price that there would be some action taken by
the city regarding the police coming to his home. Mr. Quimby

- 2 -

stated that neither he or his wife desired to press any charges
against Officers Ashby or Molnar. He stated that when they
entered his home, the officers had no criminal intent against
he or his wife or property and he thought they were alert in
noticing that the lights were on in his home knowing that he
had just been married and believing he was on his honeymoon.
The officers were advised that either Public Works Supervisor
Steve Morton or Assistant City Manager Gary Price must be
the complainant in this matter along with the City Manager.

For further information in regards to Mr. Quimby, please read
this attached statement.

Investigation indicates that Officers Ashby and Molnar were
detailed at 12:01 a.m., Sunday, October 16, 1983, to the home of
City Employee Doug Quimby to ascertain if the suspect in the firing
of a weapon at a police officer, Don Howze, may be at this residence.
Information received was that Howze worked with Quimby at the
Public Works Department, City of Sanibel and that he, (Howze), was
a friend of Quimby's and may be at his home as it was in the
vicinity of the reported shooting. Quimby had just been married
on Saturday, October 15, and was a personal friend of Officer Molnar,
who had known Quimby since being on the island. Knowing that
Quimby was just married, and observing the lights and TV on at the
Quimby apartment, and believing that Quimby was on his honeymoon,
they thought this to be unusual. As they had reasonable grounds to
believe that the newly-married couple were not at home and that
the suspect, who in the past has been convicted of felony charges
of concealed firearm, and assaults on Police Officers, may be at
this address, the officers obtained a key and permission of the
landlord, Dave Wooster, who lives across the hall from the Quimby
apartment, to check out the apartment. Wooster stated he did not
know the location of the Quimbys. The officers knocked on the
door and received no response. They then entered the apartment
with the key obtained from the landlord and observed Mrs. Quimby
in the hallway outside the bathroom and Mr. Quimby watching TV.
They did not threaten the Quimbys or point any weapons at them.
They explained the reason for being at Quimby's home, apologized
for the inconvenience and left.

Standard Operating Procedure for all Police Officers, when
attempting to apprehend or locate an armed suspect, is to have
their weapons in their hand; in this matter, one officer had a
shotgun and the other his service revolver. It should be noted to
your office that many police officers are killed yearly because
they fear they should not draw their weapons as the wanted subject
may not be the right subject they are attempting to locate. If
the wanted person in this reported shooting incident had been
at the Quimby apartment and had wounded or killed one of our
officers, we would be asking, "Why didn't they have their weapons
drawn?"

At approximately 12:10 a.m. on the same night of this incident,
Sgt. Case and I went to the home of Sue Baird, former city employee

- 3 -

and friend of Don Howze, with information that she had just
been with Howze. When I went to the Sue Baird home, I had
my weapon drawn and in my hand. If for some reason your
office feels this is an improper police action (police officers
drawing weapons when attempting to locate armed suspect), please
advise your recommendations for a procedure to handle this type
of a situation.

I am enclosing for your review:

1. Complaint No. 5354-83 - Complaint against officers

2. Your memorandum reference unauthorized entry - and drawn weapons.

3. Response of Officer Ashby and Police Report

4. Reponse of Officer Molnar and Police Report

5. Statement of George Douglas Quimby

Complaints and Investigation 17.8 (A)

As the Chief of Police City of Sanibel (Department Director), I
find that no further investigation is warranted in this matter.
This finding is based on the above stated facts, a review of
State-Federal Laws, City Ordinances, Sanibel Police Policy and
Rules and Regulations, City of Sanibel PERSONNEL MANAGEMENT SYSTEM.

Under Section E, City of Sanibel PERSONNEL MANAGEMENT SYSTEM,
"Where the activities being investigated involve possible
criminal activity on the part of any City employee", I will discuss
this matter with you personally.

John P. Butler
Chief of Police

MEMORANDUM

DATE: October 18, 1983

TO: Police Chief

FROM: City Manager

RE: Your Memorandum of October 18 in Response
            to my Memorandum of October 17

I am in receipt of your Memorandum and have reviewed it in
its entirety. I have a number of questions and it is my
intention to discuss them with you upon my return from
vacation. In the meantime, I am asking the City Attorney
and Acting City Manager Price for their comments.

However, I do not want to wait until my return from vacation
to express my extreme disappointment in your treating this as
a complaint against Officers Molnar and Ashby, or for that
matter anyone else in your department. Because of this
extreme concern, I am taking the liberty of copying your
Memo to Officer Ashby, Officer Molnar, Sergeant Case, Sergeant
Blackmore and Mr. and Mrs. Quimby.

If you read my memo more carefully, you would have noted that
I merely asked you to provide me with an explanation and
information surrounding the events of that alleged incident.
I am perfectly within my responsibilities and rights to inquire
about any departmental activity. To do otherwise would be
irresponsible and an abdication of my responsibility and
authority. So please be advised that when similar situations
in the future occur, I will request and expect a report and
explanation from your office.

I have a great deal of confidence in Officer Molnar and
Officer Ashby and I very much resent the implication that I
have brought complaints against them, or for that matter am
conducting an investigation as to their involvement.

At the time I wrote the memo to you, I did not know who the
officers were nor did I know during our heated discussion in
my office. I merely asked you as a Department Director
to provide me with a report about the matter that may have
been innocuous, but may also have been very serious.

Police Chief
Page Two
October 18, 1983

At this point no one is under investigation and there are
no complaints against any officers. Please make this very
clear to all participants.

I also want to make very clear to you that the Quimbys
were not in any manner complainants.   In fact, I was told
that they were not complaining; but I did choose to ask you
for a report because I thought the matter may have
some serious and improper overtones to it.   Please note
that I said may have and please be reminded that I believe
it to be my responsibility to look into any such matter
in any department at any time.

With further regard to the Quimbys, I think it would have
been more proper for you to discuss the matter more fully
with me as to the source of my information. Also, when I am
asking you for a report in the future, I don't expect you to
treat it as an official police complaint or ask the source of
my concern until a complaint or specific charge has been made.

Every inquiry on my part should not be construed as an
official complaint or major investigation. As a Department
Director I would hope you would put these inquiries into
perspective.

We will discuss the matter more fully when I return.

Bernard J. Murphy, Jr.,
City Manager

BJM:VJS

cc: City Attorney David LaCroix
      Acting City Manager Gary A. Price
      Sergeant Case
      Sergeant Blackmore
      Officer Molnar
      Officer Ashby
      Mr. and Mrs. Douglas Quimby

THE POLICE SHOULD USE A LITTLE MORE DISCRETION

Despite the community's strong support of the SPD, and scores of letters praising its performance, islanders were not always overjoyed by our response to their complaints. For it never occurred to people who called about cars speeding in their neighborhoods that the vast majority of those subsequently cited for speeding would be local residents and, quite frequently, themselves.

Not surprisingly, many residents who received speeding tickets were utterly outraged. "You ought to be out catching the bad guys instead of picking on law-abiding citizens!" they cried. Others, like Denny (not his real name), advised the officer who stopped him for speeding that he was paying his salary and was a close friend of people in high places in city government.

Denny didn't like the officer who cited him for speeding. The ex-Marine also disliked Officer Applegate, who cited him for his contribution to a traffic accident. And when Officer Ashby questioned his daughter about some police matter, the hot-tempered salesman added Ashby to his growing list of arrogant cops in dire need of the kind of attitude adjustment he would be delighted to administer.

As Chief of the SPD, I knew it was only a matter of time until Denny found fault with me.

* * *

Denny and I were on friendly terms, a rapport based primarily upon certain common denominators. We both came from the Midwest, were bigger than most men (but not each other), and had an Irish-Catholic background. Several years in the Marine Corps had rendered us fluent in the vulgate version of the English language - always colorful, often unprintable.

Denny was already convinced that we were doing what we were *not* paid to do: harass island residents. Thus, when local newspapers published the irate letter of a resident the SPD had cited for violating the parking ordinance, Denny blew a gasket. After all, the police were supposed to issue parking tickets to tourists, not law-abiding citizens.

Enacted in 1981, the parking ordinance was the city's response to citizen complaints. Residents of the Gumbo Limbo subdivision complained that tourists hogged all the parking places at public beach accesses. Residents of W. Gulf Drive complained that tourists parked on the right of way and trespassed en route to the Gulf of Mexico. Therefore, the ordinance made it illegal to park on any right of way, and restricted parking at certain beach accesses.

Unfortunately, the city ordinance was impossible to enforce. For the only way the SPD could legally collect parking fines from non-residents who ignored them was to present them with a Notice to Appear in court. Moreover, said Notice could not be sent by registered mail. The court required us to deliver it in person to the long-gone scofflaw, who often lived several thousand miles away.

But in my eyes, the most frustrating aspect of the parking ordinance was not the fact that it was unenforceable. For in police work, unenforceable laws go with the territory. Rather, the most frustrating aspect of the ordinance was the fact that it infuriated everyone cited for violating it. As a result, the SPD bore the full brunt of their righteous wrath.

Outraged tourists considered the hefty fine a form of highway robbery, for which the SPD was entirely responsible. People involved in Sanibel's lucrative tourist industry blamed us for ruining visitors' vacations and giving $anibel a bad name. Winter residents cited for parking at the wrong "residential" beach access became apoplectic with rage, and everyone complained about the confusing signs and their improper placement.

But in addition to being a no-win proposition, the parking ordinance left the SPD firmly impaled on the horns of a dilemma, a.k.a. damned if you do, damned if you don't. And since Denny made a point of keeping tabs on our damnable dilemmas, I wasn't at all surprised when he called me at the station. For periodically, Denny felt it was his duty as a friend and former gyrene to inform me that Sanibel's taxpayers were extremely displeased with the SPD.

Bracing myself for a litany of complaints, unsolicited advice for my own good, and the friendly exchange of foul language, I picked up the phone.

* * *

"Hey Denny, what's happening?"

"Hi there, old buddy! Uh - you busy right now?"

That was tough question to answer. For like most islanders, Denny believed that the police should *always* be busy catching day trippers violating our ordinances, but *never* too busy to respond to a citizen's complaint about an alligator in the back yard or a snake in the toilet bowl. Therefore, I assured Denny that I was indeed busy, but not too busy to talk to him.

"So what's on your mind?" I asked, strongly suspecting it wouldn't be wildlife.

"What's on my mind? Christ, John, didn't you see that letter in the paper from the guy who got the parking ticket?"

"We've got copies of all the parking tickets, Denny. Which one are you talking about?"

"I think his name is Flinton. Anyway, I read his letter and called him up because it really pissed me off. And I'm telling you, John, this guy is mad as hell at the police!"

While it pissed *me* off that Denny had called the man in question, I wasn't surprised, for he never missed a chance to commiserate with anyone who was mad at the SPD. However, I put my temper on temporary hold and tried to recall recent complaints about parking citations.

"You say his name is Flinton? I think he's the one who told us the sign was confusing, or in the wrong place, or whatever the hell. He got his money back, didn't he?"

"Yeah. But for Christ's sake, he's sixty-three years old and retired two years out of Ohio. Just how the hell threatening can a guy like this be?" Clearly, Denny wasn't about to be mollified.

"What can I tell you? We were wrong on the damn thing. But it's just that, no matter how hard you try, you can't do everything in this job perfectly, Denny. You know the ones who wanted this fucking parking ordinance are you people who live on Sanibel! *You* are the ones who wanted that son of bitch! *You* are the ones who call up and complain about the cars. The Police Department has no control over the signs."

Denny decided to back off a bit. "I know that, old buddy, I'm just telling you for your own good that the police should use a little bit of discretion."

"You're absolutely right, Denny. But, you can't brainwash every individual. I've told everyone in this Police Department that when someone comes to the station with a parking ticket and they have any kind of excuse - their wife had to piss and go in the bushes, the tire was flat, the mother-in-law was sick, they had to look for the kids on the beach, they didn't see the sign, the sign was improperly placed - *Excuse the ticket!*"

"Well if that's the case, John, how come your people gave this guy Flinton such a hard time?"

"Because I can't be here twenty-four hours a day and hold these people's hands! *That's* the problem, and I just don't know how to get around it."

Having shot myself in the foot by admitting there was a problem I couldn't solve, Denny immediately seized the opportunity to tell me how to solve it, "There is a way," he began, as though announcing the Second Coming.

"What's that?" I asked, feeling wary rather than receptive. For during the past quarter-century, scores of citizens had tried to tell me how to do my job. Their law-enforcement credentials were generally based on the fact that their incomes were far superior to mine, which presumably rendered their knowledge of police work far superior to mine.

"Look," Denny continued, "let me tell you something. I was in the ten fuckin' million dollar club last year, okay? Now the reason I'm telling you that is because there's a way to do things with people and a way not to do them. But what's happening is that the arrogance of certain police officers is getting out of hand. I mean, even people at city hall are starting to complain about it! And when I was at the Lions Club meeting the other night, Lefty told me..."

While Denny rambled on about Lefty and the Lions, I ruminated over his reference to city hall. For during my years as Chief of the SPD, I'd served under six city managers and received strong support from the council (whose five elected members generally survived far longer than the non-elected city managers). And although the SPD had frequently been involved with members of city hall in an official capacity, the latter never complained about the manner in which the police tried to prevent public exposure of their personal problems and peccadilloes.

When a councilman complained that his daughter had run off with a black man, we located her in a seedy section of New Orleans. When the assistant city manager's estranged wife complained that he was constantly threatening her, I had a little chat with him. And when an officer on night patrol saw a married councilman mounted like a beached whale on someone else's wife, he never reported that illegal, adulterous act.

However, the SPD couldn't avoid investigating city employees suspected of using dope or dipping into the till. Nor could we legally refrain from arresting council members' adult children caught selling dope or burglarizing homes.

* * *

Doubtless delighted to monopolize my attention for so long without being interrupted, Denny never realized my mind had wandered. For when I tuned backed in, he was still on the same subject.

"Lefty's a hell of a guy, John - lives over in Shell Harbor. You know him?"

"I know him. I went over to his house and talked with him about the incident and..."

"You did? Well, I've got news for you," said Denny, who then paused for full dramatic effect. "Lefty is fucking livid!"

"Yeah? Well, I know he got stopped by a policeman..."

"Leanos. Leanos went bumper to bumper with him all the way down Periwinkle! What kind of bullshit is that?"

"Look, Denny, I already talked to him about that. Leanos says the guy was weaving; the guy says he wasn't. Now, if *you* were chief of police, would you tell your officers not to stop anyone for weaving? Because if you tell them not to do it, they won't do it. But if some driver weaving down Periwinkle hits a tree, kills a kid, or runs over a tourist, the shit will really hit the fan when word gets out that you gave the orders not to stop..."

"But you're missing the point, old buddy. Nobody's saying you shouldn't stop people who aren't driving the way they should be. I'm just telling you, as a friend, that the police should use a little more discretion. I mean, this isn't Miami or Philadelphia or Newark, John. The cops here don't have it tough, and..."

"Yeah," I cut in, "but all you gotta do is have one incident and *then* you've got it tough."

"Have you ever had it close?" Denny asked, suddenly sounding more like a gyrene than an irate citizen.

"You better believe we've had it close!" I said, eager to tell him what policing paradise was *really* like. "How about the guy who broke into..."

"How about *your* guys that broke into Quimby's apartment with their fuckin' guns out?" Denny interrupted, clearly more interested in arguing than listening. (People in high places must have passed the word.)

"They did exactly right, Denny. I'm telling you, baby, it was done exactly right. You come talk to me about that sometime."

But the salesman didn't want to talk to me about SOP when seeking an armed suspect. Rather, he wanted to tell me, as a friend, that certain islanders were increasingly unhappy with the SPD in general and certain policemen in particular.

"You know, I'm not looking for trouble," he began, "but I get around this town a good bit. Now, I'm going to tell you something," Denny announced in his Second Coming voice: "There is criticism against the Sanibel Police Department and it is mounting!"

Pausing long enough to let the full impact of his pronouncement penetrate the thick skull of a police chief (who'd never belonged to the ten million dollar club) Denny reverted to his non-celestial voice. "I'm just telling you this for your own good, old buddy of mine."

"I understand," I said to that good old buddy of mine - who frequently fanned the fires of discontent. Encouraged by my understanding, Denny proceeded to tell me precisely what was wrong with the SPD.

"It's the arrogance of some of the cops down here. Like that guy - uh, Ashby - who questioned my daughter in front of all her employees and other people and embarrassed the shit out of her. That's not smart, John. You don't have to be a genius to be a policeman, but...Jesus Christ, use a little bit of discretion! After all, this is a resort - **THIS IS A FUCKING RESORT!"**

"I understand that," I replied, ignoring the dumb-cop remark in the hope of ending an X-rated conversation that was undoubtedly burning up the telephone wires at city hall. But, once again, my understanding merely encouraged Denny to vent his spleen.

"This ain't Newark, John. I mean, you get a couple of niggers shooting at you - *then* you got a problem. See what I'm saying?"

"Yeah...but the police can run into the same thing down here," I countered.

"*What?*" screamed the salesman. "Being a cop on Sanibel is like being a bishop in the fucking Catholic Church!"

That was too much. "Now you just listen!" I shouted. "When I first came here, I've got Don Hiers with a gun at my head. *That's* fucking Newark. When Betty Weir got those two dope addicts up at Wegryn's clinic and they were both on heroin, where the hell is that? Is that Newark, or is that Sanibel? And when the guys down at..."

"Yeah but..."

"Just wait a minute, Denny. You don't know everything that goes on here. All you know is what people tell you and what you read in the paper. How about the guys we just got breaking into the Lighthouse Restaurant? The fucking kid's got hepatitis or something. And how about the time before we caught 'em and they've got some other damn communicable disease?"

"Look Denny," I continued, "we're sure as hell not perfect. And, believe me, I'm doing my best to correct anything we're doing wrong. But as the Department grows, it becomes more difficult to have these people function the way I want them to function: good common horse sense…"

"And a hell of a lot more discretion with residents," Denny added.

"That, too," I quickly agreed. "In fact, I've been thinking about how to do this. Maybe we should put a big, neon sticker on everyone's license plate. That way, when we stop you, we'll know you're from Sanibel. Case closed!"

Now roaring with laughter rather than rage, Denny took a few moments to catch his breath before commenting on my suggestion. "Sounds like a great idea," he chuckled. "Maybe if you do that, your guys will use a little more discretion with the people who pay their salaries!"

"You're absolutely right, Denny, no question about it. You people pay our wages here. You do that and so does Lefty - or whatever the hell his name is."

"Lefty. He's a hell of a guy. You know him?"

"Yeah. Isn't he the one who had open-heart surgery and ran around in that little electric car?"

"Right. And he doesn't drink!"

"I know that, Denny. But you and I make up for what he doesn't drink."

"That's right. But we've got to keep somebody going!"

"I sure can't argue with that. See you soon, and thanks for calling me."

"Bye, old buddy."

* * *

"To stay alive, you gotta dig all jive," I thought, hanging up the phone with a sigh of relief. Although I'd heard that expression years ago in an entirely different connection, I felt it applied to police work more than any other profession. For a policeman's effectiveness, and frequently his very survival, are largely dependent upon his ability to communicate with all kinds of people in every conceivable (and inconceivable) situation.

In one respect, however, Denny was right: serious crime was certainly far less prevalent on Sanibel than in Newark, New Jersey. But he was dead wrong to compare a Sanibel police officer to a bishop in the expletive-deleted Catholic Church. For the SPD dealt with robberies and burglaries, murders and suicides, pornography and prostitution, drugs and domestic disputes, a plethora of wildlife complaints and, in one case, a dire threat to blow up the causeway.

Yet I remained disturbed by Denny's repeated references to arrogant cops and mounting criticism of the SPD. Moreover, I knew only too well that donning the uniform of a police officer sometimes transformed a decent civilian into a swaggering, arrogant cop.

But since letters of commendation continued to pour in, it certainly seemed that the vast majority of people on Sanibel were thoroughly satisfied with the SPD. And since I'd always believed that a police department is really run by the people - not the chief, the city council, or the mayor - such a steady outpouring of public support proved extremely reassuring.

However, it soon became clear that Sanibel's new city manager had different ideas about who really ran the SPD - and how it should be run.

Results of questionnaire

BASED ON TOTAL OF 372 RESPONDENTS

1. Please rate the overall performance of each of the following.

	Excellent	Good	Fair	Poor	No Answer
a. Sanibel City Council	12%	48%	30%	9%	2%
b. Sanibel City Administration	5	38	33	20	4
c. Sanibel Planning Commission	10	36	28	21	5
d. Sanibel Police Department	50	36	9	2	4

2. **A comprehensive** land use plan was developed to protect Sanibel's natural **resources, yet** permitting planned residential and commercial development.

	Excellent	Good	Fair	Poor	No Answer
How good of a job is the City of Sanibel doing in meeting this goal?	8%	35%	38%	18%	1%

3. Would you agree or disagree with each of the following statements?

	Strongly Agree	Agree	Disagree	Strongly Disagree	No Answer
a. City taxes on Sanibel Island are reasonable	12%	58%	19%	7%	4%
b. The City of Sanibel should undertake a major road building and improvement program	19	23	34	22	1
c. The City of Sanibel should continue to make moderate priced housing available on Sanibel Island	13	23	25	36	2
d. The City of Sanibel should build a new City Hall	6	23	35	33	4
e. The causeway should be owned by the City of Sanibel	31	34	13	19	3

4. Comments

5. Do you live on Sanibel....

More than six months a year	95%
Less than six months a year	1
Do not live on Sanibel	2
No Answer	2

6. How long have you lived on Sanibel?

Less than one year	5%
One - five years	39
Six - ten years	38
More than ten years	16
No Answer	2

7. Are you registered to vote on Sanibel?

Yes	93%
No	6
No Answer	1

POLITICS IN PARADISE

Not long after City Manager Bernie Murphy resigned, he was replaced by his assistant in the fall of '84. For as the council subsequently explained to the public, Gary Price knew far more about Sanibel than did any other candidate. Moreover, the council felt that Price's several years of work with the city certainly qualified him—indeed entitled him—to receive the promotion. Thus, despite my past disagreements with Gary over numerous police problems, I hoped he would recognize the value of training and motivating SPD personnel.

A police chief's most important job is to select, train and, above all, motivate his personnel. Without motivation, no amount of training will make a policeman a good public servant - or prevent him from becoming a bad one. For whether his work is highly superior or barely average, he receives the same salary on pay day.

During my twenty years as a police chief, public recognition proved to be one of the most effective means of motivation - and it never cost the taxpayers a penny. The publication of citizens' letters of appreciation was always a winner, for publicizing an officer's outstanding performance pleased him and his family tremendously. It also let the public know that members of their tax-supported police department were doing a good job.

Providing opportunities for advanced training was another effective form of motivation. Officers Ray Rhodes and Lew Phillips had successfully completed intensive, three-month programs at the prestigious National FBI Academy and the Southern Police Institute. In fact, Phillips held the remarkable distinction of graduating first in his class at *both* institutions.

Unfortunately, it soon became clear that my new boss wasn't at all interested in motivating members of the SPD. Indeed, he took an exceedingly dim view of the favorable publicity we received. Thus, in the spring of '85, Gary Price ordered me not to release any more letters of commendation or appreciation to the press. While I promptly complied with the city manager's directive concerning "attaboy" letters, I began to give some thought to retirement.

Subsequently, during the course of general conversation, I asked Gary if he had anyone in mind to replace me when I retired. While Price replied that he had no particular person in mind, he made it perfectly clear that my successor would *not* be anyone in the SPD. Capt. Rhodes was "too immature" and Lt. Phillips was "too macho," he said.

I was deeply disturbed by the realization that neither Ray nor Lew would be promoted. Sanibel's citizens had paid for their advanced, professional training, both men had served the SPD for over ten years, and contributed to the community in ways that went well beyond the call of duty. Since highly qualified personnel who are denied the promotions they deserve frequently find employment elsewhere, I feared that Sanibel's loss would be another city's gain.

Therefore, I decided to hang in there a while and wait for the city manager to follow the example of all his predecessors, i.e., leave Sanibel sooner rather than later. But in 1987, Price made it perfectly clear that he had no intention of leaving the city - and every intention of getting rid of me.

January: Citizen Discontent

"Now is the winter of our discontent" best describes the mood of many islanders in 1987. Indeed, the year began with community outrage over several amendments to the ordinance that regulated occupational licenses - changes that affected everyone from the Avon Lady to the boy next door, who supplemented his allowance by mowing lawns. For anyone engaged in any kind of "business" on

Sanibel (except a garage sale), must have an occupational license.

One amendment required licensees to be "of good moral character," and empowered the city manager to determine whether or not they were. Another amendment enabled the city manager to revoke occupational licenses by acting as enforcer, prosecutor and judge. But the most egregious violation of constitutional rights was the amendment authorizing the city manager, or his designees, to inspect the premises of licensees and review their records "with or without a search warrant."

Yet while scores of licensees were appalled by these amendments, most feared that public opposition would mark them for retaliation. But armed with the courage of their convictions, five long-time businessmen decided to file a class-action suit against the city.*

However, dissatisfaction was by no means limited to the business community. Indeed, numerous citizens had come to me with complaints about city employees - particularly some in the powerful planning department. In addition to "negative attitude," they cited examples of abusive treatment and the planning department's alleged failure to afford them due process of law.

In view of the brouhaha over the occupational license, the city manager was well aware of the business community's discontent. Indeed, I had informed him of the pending lawsuit. However, it occurred to me that Price might not be fully aware of islanders' increasing dissatisfaction with some of their public servants.

Thus, despite the fact that every policeman in his right mind avoids politics like the plague, it was clearly my duty to inform my civilian superior of the mounting unrest among the citizenry he served. The perfect opportunity to do so presented itself early the following month.

February: Retire, or Be Fired

Gary Price saw me walking by his office on February 9 and invited me in. Since City Attorney David LaCroix happened to be present, I considered the city manager's invitation a golden opportunity to

---

* The lawsuit, which named the city manager and City Attorney LaCroix as defendants, challenged the constitutionality of the occupational license ordinance. The city subsequently agreed to delete the most offensive portions of the ordinance.

discuss citizen complaints with two of the most powerful people on Sanibel. While unaware that February 9,1987 was Price's fortieth birthday, I doubt that such knowledge would have made any difference.

Following a few minutes of general conversation, I advised Gary and David of the growing unrest among islanders and the precise nature of their complaints. However, someone who presents a problem should also offer a solution. Thus, I suggested the possibility of sending cards to a random selection of people who had dealings with city hall, asking whether they had been treated in a courteous, professional manner.

Such cards, I reasoned, would serve a dual purpose: they would make citizens feel that the city *cared* about the kind of treatment they received, and also reveal which employees needed to be reminded that they were public servants. But as Price insisted that no PR problem existed, I lost my Irish temper, the city attorney beat a hasty retreat, and I engaged in a heated argument with the city manager.

I informed Gary that a retired policeman from Pennsylvania, who was quitting his job in the planning department, had told me that they treated murderers in Philadelphia better than the planning department treated people on Sanibel. The department enforced beliefs and prejudices rather than the law, I maintained, and offered a solution to that problem, too. The next time Price left me in charge as acting city manager, something he had done over a dozen times, I would fire Planning Director Bruce Rogers.

Ten days later, the city manager handed me (without comment), a large, interdepartmental envelope. Its contents clearly constituted an ultimatum: if I didn't retire immediately, Gary Price would fire me immediately. Specifically, the envelope contained the following documents:

(1) Price's draft of an official press release (undated and unsigned), stating that John Butler had been fired because "his attitude and performance are not of the quality we want for employees of the City and he has consistently shown an unwillingness to work as a team with the citizens, City Council, and other City departments."

(2) An unsigned Note-O-Gram (dated February 18), specifying that I would receive $5,467.86 in accrued sick leave and $1,352 in bonus pay - if I retired immediately.

(3) Price's draft of a letter concerning the February 9 discussion with him and City Attorney LaCroix, complaining about my "childish outbreak" and expressing grave doubts about my ability to remain in charge of the SPD.

(4) A Performance Evaluation form in which Price rated me a low to moderately satisfactory employee, the only time I'd ever received less than an excellent rating during my twelve years as Chief of the SPD.

Although stunned by Price's interdepartmental communication, its contents "persuaded" me to retire - for the refusal to do so would jeopardize my pension. But quite apart from the financial considerations, I realized that I couldn't continue to work for a city manager who didn't appear to care about the people in the community he served.

Therefore, and without even consulting my wife (a first in our many years of married life), I announced my retirement in a letter to Gary Price dated February 19 - one day after my twelfth anniversary as Chief of the SPD. "It has been a pleasure serving the City of Sanibel, its citizens and visitors, but my time has come to step down."

The city manager immediately accepted my retirement letter. "Dear John," he wrote the following day, "It is with sincere sorrow that I accept your notice of retirement. As the most senior City employee, the first to be hired by the fledgling community, your leaving marks the passing of an era."

March: "Just who is in charge at the SPD?"

While islanders had no reason to question "the passing of an era," the city manager's decision to look outside the SPD for my successor met with widespread, public criticism. In a letter to local newspapers, the venerable Arthur Hunter eloquently expressed the views of many Sanibel citizens. "I venture there is no police department anywhere of higher excellence. It seems to me important that every effort possible be made to extend this era by the appointment of a new chief of police from within the carefully selected, highly trained, competent, dedicated and honest top people in the existing staff."

But in mid-March, the *Islander* reported that Capt. Ray Rhodes, "long considered the most logical successor to Chief John Butler," was leaving the SPD to become Director of Public Safety in Gladstone, Missouri. Editor Cindy Chalmers went on to explain that Rhodes began looking elsewhere "when it became apparent that he was not in line for the chief's job on Sanibel."

Later in her lengthy article, Chalmers wondered, "Just who is in charge at the SPD?" For as she correctly reported, I hoped to use up accumulated vacation time prior to my actual retirement in July, Capt. Bill Trefny was recovering from open-heart surgery, and Capt. Rhodes would be leaving the SPD before the end of the month. Even ranking Sgt. Jack Primm, she noted, was expected to be hospitalized for several weeks. But the editor didn't know the real story behind his hospitalization.

Early in March, Primm called from out of state and told me that he'd just resigned from the National FBI Academy. Highly distraught, Jack explained that if he hadn't resigned, the Academy would have expelled him for alcohol abuse, and harassing a female officer - charges he didn't deny.

I urged Jack to come right home, check into Charter Glade (Fort Myers' "specialty" hospital), and then call both City Manager Gary Price and Mayor Fred Valtin. Fortunately, Primm followed my advice. But so far as I was concerned, his career as a police officer was finished.

In my experience, any officer who brought disgrace and disrespect upon his department was invariably severely punished - and generally terminated. In this particular instance, however, such proved not to be the case. For Primm had a friend in high places: the city manager. Indeed, Price and Primm were close friends.

The city manager and Mayor Valtin decided not to punish or reprimand Primm. In fact, they didn't even require him to apologize for his behavior. They simply gave him a contract to sign, which stipulated that he would keep his nose clean and reimburse the public monies used to send him to the FBI Academy.

Not surprisingly, since I was in the process of going 10-7 (out of service), Price and Valtin didn't speak with me on this matter, which was just as well. I would never have agreed with them.

April: The Town Meeting

The powers that be succeeded in keeping the problem of a particular police officer under wraps. However, the local press continued to write about citizen dissatisfaction with the city manager's decision to conduct a nationwide search for my replacement.

Thus, in an article announcing Lew Phillips' application for the position, the *Island Reporter's* Matt Perez introduced the subject by stating that both islanders and members of the SPD felt there was no need to look outside the city for the next chief. Perez quoted Price: "Just because I'm going outside doesn't mean that I'm going to hire outside." (But he subsequently did.)

In an effort to put the SPD question to rest, Sanibel's city council, under the strong leadership of Mayor Valtin, made a very wise move: they held an old-fashioned town meeting. In addition to the SPD, the agenda included several topics that citizens had previously submitted for discussion. As a result, the Community Center was packed on the night of April 9.

Mayor Valtin began the meeting by asking people who'd lived on Sanibel for more than twenty-five years to raise their hands, and made most gracious comments about those who did. He then repeated this process with members of the audience who had been here more than twenty, fifteen, ten, and five years. And when Valtin eventually asked relatively new residents to raise their hands, he warmly welcomed them to Sanibel.

While a few disgruntled citizens grumbled about the mayor's waste of time, the vast majority were immensely pleased by his time-consuming preliminaries. For since nearly all adult "islanders" are born and raised somewhere else, they take great pride in their residential longevity, and welcome any public opportunity to reveal the precise length of their pedigree. Thus, when the mayor finally turned the first item on the agenda over to the city manager, the audience was in an extremely good mood.

Gary Price read a two-page statement concerning the SPD. In reference to my retirement and Capt. Rhodes' departure, the city manager explained that "the recent events in the Department have been a coincidental culmination of a series of independent events...over which no one had control." However, he quickly assured the audience, "there is no emergency" and, he added, "no voids will be created."

Price devoted the second half of his prepared statement to outlining various procedures he planned to follow in hiring Sanibel's next police chief. "I will head a committee of approximately 10 interested citizens to participate in the selection process" was a real winner. Few people realized that the man who headed the committee of citizen volunteers would also be instrumental in selecting its members.

Following Price's presentation, Mayor Valtin resumed control of the meeting and moved to other topics on the agenda. Apart from outbursts by a few irate citizens, most people seemed to feel that they'd seen democracy in action - and were reassured by the results.

Things calmed down considerably after the April 9 town meeting. The local press stopped writing about the SPD, the last of Sanibel's visiting "snowbirds" migrated back to their northern residences, and scores of islanders prepared for *their* annual migration to northern climes during the summer months.

Thus, the Sanibel Police Department ceased to be a topic of either public concern or conversation. But an unexpected visitor caused me to change my mind about going out like a lamb.

May: Now It's My Turn

The visitor in question was an investigative reporter from the Fort Myers *News-Press*. He dropped by my office one day and, following a few minutes of general conversation, suddenly asked a mind-boggling question: "Chief, did you ever think that the reason they asked you to retire was because you arrested the mayor's kid?"*

* A stepson, who pleaded guilty to burglary.

While the reporter proceeded to mention other members of the mayor's family, with whom the SPD had been obliged to deal, my mind wandered elsewhere. Specifically, back to Mansfield, Ohio and the memorable explosion of July 4, 1948.

Responding to a call about a break-in at a particular building, my partner and I arrived at the back door. But instead of finding a burglar, we found several sticks of dynamite taped together - and a fizzling fuse. "Holy shit!" was doubtless my last coherent thought before a tremendous explosion caused parts of the building to collapse upon us. Although remarkably intact when rescued from the rubble, we spent some time in the hospital.

Prior to the reporter's visit, I'd viewed that past explosion in Ohio and my recent "retirement" from the SPD in the same light: events over which I had no control, and couldn't fight. But after the reporter left my office, I gave considerable thought to what he'd said and reached the following conclusions: (1) the city manager would never have presented me a retire-or-be-fired ultimatum without the mayor's consent, (2) it was now my turn to fight Sanibel's city hall.

However, and for reasons best known to themselves, attorneys on Sanibel shy away from doing battle with the city. Therefore, I went to Fort Myers and discussed the situation with Patrick Geraghty, Esq. of Henderson, Franklin, Starnes & Holt. I also showed him the retire-or-be-fired documents Price had included in his interdepartmental envelope. Pat Geraghty didn't hesitate to take on the case.

Thus, on May 18, my lawyer wrote to both City Manager Price and Mayor Valtin informing them that I'd rescinded my retirement letter and intended to resume my duties as head of the SPD on a full-time basis. For after conferring with me, Geraghty went on to explain, "it appears that the circumstances leading to the submission of his retirement letter dated February 19 were anything but 'voluntary' and were in possible violation of Florida Statute 112.3187."

The statute in question, generally referred to as the "Whistleblowers Act," prohibits municipal employers from taking retaliatory actions against employees who report alleged violations of law by their employers or colleagues. But since the statute had been on the books for less than a year, no case had yet been tried under its provisions. Thus, when Price refused to accept the formal withdrawal of my retirement, the press had a field day.

The *Islander* quoted from Price's letter to Geraghty: "I do not feel that his retirement was involuntary."

The *News-Press* quoted Geraghty: "I don't feel when you have a gun to your head that you can make a legitimate decision."

The *Island Reporter* quoted me: "It's goddamn near extortion what he did."

At the end of the month, the city manager informed both the *Islander* and the *Reporter* that my retirement would go into effect July 26, as scheduled, and that advertisements for a new chief of police were already being run in professional publications. In connection with possible violations of the Whistleblowers Act, Price's prepared statement was unequivocal:

> "I am aware of no instance in which the police chief has reported violations of law, or any improper practice or procedure, or any ethical violation, or any act of malfeasance, misfeasance, or neglect of duty on the part of any city employee, department or contractor."

Therefore, I began compiling a list of reported incidents that I considered to be acts of malfeasance, misfeasance, or neglect of duty on Price's part. But before Pat Geraghty and I finalized the list, the city manager and the planning director came under attack from a different quarter: a special report in the *Islander*.

June: Pandora's Box

After hearing countless, off-the-record complaints from people about their treatment at city hall, Editor Chalmers decided that increasing citizen dissatisfaction was a story that needed to be told. Fearing retaliation, few citizens volunteered to speak on the record. But the five who did really blasted Gary Price and Bruce Rogers.

Published June 16, "You Can't Fight City Hall" opened Pandora's Box. Mayor Valtin's response was both immediate and reassuring: "We can't continue to live with this. We must find a solution," he told the press.

Like Sanibel's first Mayor, Fred Valtin formerly worked for the

CIA. One of the half-dozen, ex-Company men who had held influential positions on Sanibel since incorporation, Mayor Valtin knew all about damage control. Highly intelligent and articulate, he succeeded in persuading his fellow councilmen to take the actions required to close Pandora's Box.

Foremost was council's unanimous vote of confidence in City Manager Gary Price. Subsequently, the council devoted several, special sessions to identifying other causes of public dissatisfaction with city hall, endorsed Price's proposal to provide attitude training for city employees, and appropriated $25,000 to hire a marketing firm to conduct a citizen survey.*

Coincidentally, my lawyer filed suit against the City of Sanibel, City Manager Gary Price and City Attorney David LaCroix shortly after the *Islander* published "You Can't Fight City Hall." Desperate for news during the dull, summer months, local papers gave the lawsuit extensive coverage. Indeed, the space devoted to Sanibel's fiftieth annual Shell Fair in March paled by comparison.

June-July: Lawsuit

In essence, the suit charged that Price had violated the Whistleblowers Act by forcing me to retire in retaliation for lodging complaints about unlawful acts and investigating allegations of unlawful acts. Of course the suit cited just a few complaints against the city manager, drawn from the list of eighteen that Geraghty and I had prepared. Chief among them were the following:

(1) *Misuse of state revenue-sharing funds*

When Price became city manager, he made Dick Noon (then an SPD officer), Director of Parks and Recreation - a full-time job. However, and in violation of state law, Price continued to carry Noon on the SPD pension program and Noon continued to receive police incentive pay. Although I informed Gary of these discrepancies, he or-

---

* "The Strategic Study of the Preferences and Opinions of the Citizens of Sanibel" finally arrived at city hall in the fall of 1988. To no one's surprise, it revealed considerable dissatisfaction with particular city departments and high-ranking public servants. However, *over ninety percent* of the voters were satisfied with the performance of the SPD.

dered me to sign an application for revenue sharing. I refused, and reported the violation to the Florida Department of Law Enforcement.*

(2) *Ignoring citizen complaints*

Although I'd advised the city manager of numerous complaints about the planning department (which allegedly enforced beliefs and prejudices rather than the law and failed to afford due process of law), Price never took any action regarding those complaints.

(3) *Questioning the need for an investigation*

The SPD investigated a complaint filed by Renee Rosen against her former partner, John Van Heemst. In a sworn statement, Rosen alleged that Van Heemst had paid Ken Pfalzer (a planning department employee) $24,000 for the Tree Tops Center's development permit. When advised that Van Heemst was the person who had allegedly done the bribing, Price told me the man was no good and he didn't see why the SPD should bother to investigate this matter.*

The interest generated by a lawsuit during the summer mosquito season must have encouraged the press to cover it in more detail. For local newspapers soon reported numerous other complaints against the city manager - drawn from the list of eighteen. Highlights included allegations of Price's failure to terminate a city employee who admitted the use of cocaine, his lack of immediate disciplinary actions against employee Donald Howze (a convicted felon), and his use of city lumber for lattice work around his house.

"I don't deny most of those things happened," Price told the *Reporter*, "but they're not violations of law." Then, in talking to the *Islander*, Gary called the charges against him "pathetic" and "ridiculous examples of management disagreements." Finally, when interviewed by the *News-Press*, Price responded to the suit in three words: "It's all garbage." Sanibel's city manager was not a happy camper in June.

* Following an investigation, Noon was removed from the SPD pension fund. Like Sgt. Primm, whom Price had appointed Director of the Sanibel Emergency Management Plan, Dick Noon was a close friend of the city manager.

* Since a formal complaint had been lodged, the SPD could not legally ignore it. However, our investigation uncovered no evidence to support Rosen's allegations concerning either Pfalzer or Van Heemst.

However, the following month brought him some measure of relief. For on July 15, the Lee County Sheriff's Department formally served the City of Sanibel with the civil suit Geraghty had filed in June. As a result, the press shifted its attention to City Attorney David LaCroix.

Although the city attorney had resigned, and planned to leave Sanibel in August, he gave the *Reporter* some newsworthy quotes concerning my lawsuit. "It sure makes John Butler look bad, because it's silly." And, LaCroix added, "He gave us a license to do a character assassination."

Shortly after the city attorney's comments appeared in the paper, my official retirement went into effect at midnight on July 26. On that day, I turned everything over to Capt. Bill Trefny, whom the city manager appointed Chief of the SPD the following morning - with the clear understanding that the man recuperating from open-heart surgery would retire when Gary hired my successor.

One of the documents I turned over to the interim chief was SPD Report No. 03987-87, and its several pages of attachments. The report in question was a very recent complaint against the city manager filed by Mrs. Peggy Miller (who had purchased Price's former home on Nerita Street) and her next-door neighbor, Mr. Ralph DiCarlo.

According to the complainants, Price had a boundary marker moved in order to accommodate his driveway. Neither the Millers nor the DiCarlos were aware of this alleged act until the latter obtained a survey. The complainants provided a 1978 survey indicating the original location of the boundary marker, and a 1980 survey showing its miraculous migration some twelve feet south onto the DiCarlo property.

In addition to surveys and site plans, the report included three pages of sworn testimony from Mrs. Miller. The latter alleged that an engineering firm had paid her $3,500 for a "nuisance settlement," whereby she would not sue either the firm or Gary Price.

I was glad I didn't have to investigate this latest complaint against the city manager, and wondered what Trefny would do about it.

Let's Make a Deal

Although LaCroix had regaled the press in July by saying that my lawsuit was "silly," he obviously took it seriously. For that very month, the city offered to make a deal and settle out of court. According to the proposed, amicable agreement, the city would retain me as an SPD consultant with full salary and benefits until the following February - when I'd originally planned to retire.

In return, I would drop my suit and agree to sign a document which among other things, stated that "to my knowledge, the Sanibel City government and its employees and elected officials are above reproach." The out-of-court deal also included a document for Gary Price to sign which, among other things, stated that, "John Butler has performed many years of excellent service to the City of Sanibel, and the City's Police Department, under his command, has been a great asset."

Since Price probably disliked the proposed deal as much as I did, he was undoubtedly delighted when I refused to accept it. For my suit was not a fight for reinstatement in any capacity; rather, it was a fight against injustice. However, the outgoing city attorney took an entirely different view of pending litigation that named him as a defendant. Thus, he wrote me a letter advising me that I would lose all my friends on the island if I persisted in suing the city.

But since David's letter failed to deter me from pursuing the suit, several lawyers began to dream up other deals for an out-of-court settlement. For in addition to City Attorney Bob Pritt, who had now replaced David LaCroix, the city had engaged the services of a Sarasota firm with a truly impressive number of "esquires" listed on its letterhead.

I was rather amused by a clause in one proposal, whereby I agreed not to run for city council. After all, I'd never had any intention of throwing my hat in the ring. But since the possibility clearly concerned the powers that be, they must have considered me capable of winning an election.

In any event, I viewed the proposals prepared with due, deliberate speed - legalese for a snail's pace - as stalling tactics. Indeed, one of the best ways to discourage a plaintiff from pursuing litigation is to convince him that such action will require an inordinate amount of time and an astronomical amount of money. Therefore, I instructed my attorney to move on to the discovery stage, i.e., make the necessary arrangements for depositions from the defendants.

Thus on March 16, 1988, Sanibel's city manager had the dubious pleasure of spending the entire day answering questions posed by my lawyer in the presence of the city's lawyers (City Attorney Pritt and Gregory Hootman, Esquire from the multi-esquire firm in Sarasota). By the end of the day, Gary Price had produced over two hundred pages of testimony.

Price readily agreed that the documents in the interdepartmental envelope constituted a retire-or-be-fired ultimatum. "Because," he explained, "I had intended on firing him." The city manager subsequently stated that he'd notified all council members of his decision, "but I wasn't asking them for their blessing or their approval." Indeed, nothing obliged him to do so.*

In response to questions concerning his reasons for requesting my resignation, Gary began by saying that I wasn't a "team player." After reminding the city manager that he'd made me "captain of the team" over a dozen times, Pat Geraghty asked whether any councilmen, department heads, or city employees had objected to Price's appointing me as acting city manager just two months before he decided to fire me. "No," replied the defendant, who quickly moved on to complain about my "negative attitude" toward requests from other departments to work as a team.

"Can you cite any examples of that, sir?" Geraghty inquired.

"No, I can't."

However, Price did his best to bolster his case against me by citing dissatisfaction within the SPD. "The morale of the department was in the basement" because, he said, I discouraged good officers from participating in advanced-training programs, and many officers had complained to him about being "unduly castigated" and put on unpopular shifts. However, Gary couldn't recall the name of a single

---

* According to Sanibel's charter, the elected council is not allowed to interfere with the administration, the sole province of the non-elected city manager. Moreover, the council cannot investigate the city manager's actions unless three of its five members agree to do so - without violating the Sunshine Law in the process.

officer who had complained to him. "I didn't take notes on those things," he explained.

While on the subject of complaints, Geraghty asked the city manager if he'd ever received any letters criticizing my performance. Gary didn't recall receiving any. Any letters congratulating me or the SPD? "Can't say that there were either," Price replied. At that point, Geraghty produced Exhibit No. 13: Mayor Valtin's memo expressing the highest praise for me and the SPD for our handling of the Sassman case. Gary remembered receiving a copy of the mayor's memo, written just two months before the ultimatum.

In view of what Geraghty termed the "laudatory" nature of Exhibit 13, he asked the city manager if he'd subsequently discussed his strong reservations about me with the mayor. "No, I'm sorry, I don't remember. I can't say that I did or didn't. I really don't remember."

Immediately following the city manager's deposition, Gregory Hootman (representing the Sarasota law firm) discussed a forthcoming settlement offer with my lawyer. As a result, further depositions were put on hold, whereupon Betty and I went on our long-planned vacation, providing a welcome respite from a year of pending litigation.

Unfortunately, and despite Pat Geraghty's prodding, the forthcoming offer failed to materialize during our absence. Thus, upon our return, I instructed my lawyer to notify the city's lawyers that I intended to proceed with the suit if they didn't come up with their settlement offer sooner rather than later. Otherwise, Geraghty tactfully informed his esquire counterpart in Sarasota, "it would appear to me that my client would not be in the mood to even consider a settlement proposal."

With due, deliberate speed, Gregory Hootman, Esquire finally presented the city's proposal in the summer. Naturally, subsequent negotiations proceeded at a foot-dragging pace. But the following spring, I received adequate compensation in return for signing a simple release.

Thus, two years after I began to fight city hall, the struggle was over. And contrary to LaCroix's expectations, I didn't lose my friends. For Sanibel Island is my home. I came here to stay, and I'm still here.

But in the final analysis, what really counts is not whether you won or lost—but how you played the game.

MEMORANDUM

DATE: May 10, 1985

TO: Police Chief

FROM: City Manager

RE: Letters to News Papers

I can fully understand your desire to publicize the many good things your officers do. I am just as proud of them as you are.

However, I do not think it is wise to be constantly before the public in the Letters to the Editor section of the papers. Once you establish a trend you are apt to encourage "trial by the pen" more than you should. In any case, some will still write to the paper, which can not be prevented.

On the other hand, you should not send congratulatory letters like the attached letter, unless you also send the condemnations, which none of us want to do.

Let's not have this happen in the future.

Keep up the good work.

Gary A. Price,
City Manager

GAP:VJS

Attachment

RECEIVED MAY 6 1985

May 3, 1985

Chief of Police
Sanibel Police Department
Sanibel, Flordia

Dear Sir:

I'm sorry that this letter is late in reaching you, however
Wedding plans have made my schedule somewhat hectic.

On May 7, 1984 I was the victum of a robbery on your island. I
admit to my stupidity in leaving my valuables in a place of easy access,
but none the less, the jewlery that was stolen was very special to me and
I was heart sick at its loss.

In any event I wanted you to know that the only reason I now have
my jewlery back is because of your competant police department. Officers
Leanos, Kennedy, Ashby, Hines, and Sgt. Phillips were the gentlemen I
had the chance to deal with.

The considerate manner in which they all handled the situation, in
spite of your honorable judge, was greatly appreciated. I trusted them
to do right by me and they came through.

You should be proud of your men. They wear their uniforms with a
professional aire of efficiency.

Shall be returning to Marco for our honeymoon the end of May. If
time permits we will stop over and say hello.

Thanking you again for your help and cooperation in this matter.

                              Very truly yours;

                              Jo Ann C. Testa

SANIBEL POLICE DEPARTMENT

DEPARTMENTAL DIRECTIVE

DEPARTMENTAL DIRECTIVE 54-85	DATE OF ISSUE 5/13/85	EFFECTIVE DATE 5/13/85	RESCISSION DATE
SUBJECT CHANGE IN DEPARTMENTAL POLICY POLICE COMMUNITY RELATIONS NEWS MEDIA RELATIONS			REFERENCE

A. PURPOSE

1. To inform all members that the Office of the Chief of Police has been directed by the City Manager to cease and desist forwarding letters of commendation, recognition or letters received from citizens pertaining to police actions to the news media.

2. To amend all Department Directives and Departmental Policy pertaining to release of information to the news media.

B. PROCEDURE FOR RELEASE OF POLICE DEPARTMENT INFORMATION TO NEWS MEDIA

1. All information released to the news media, including police reports, will be through the Office of the Chief of Police.

BY ORDER OF:

John P. Butler
Chief of Police

5/14/85
OK
Gary Price

cc: City Manager Price

Attd: Memo from City Manager and letter released to the news media.
SANIBEL POLICE DEPARTMENT - POLICY - Community Relations pages 9 and 10.
SANIBEL POLICE DEPARTMENT - POLICY - Community Affairs News Media Relations pages 11 and 12.

Gary Price

66 I am aware of no instance in which the police chief has reported violations of law, or any improper practice or procedure, or any ethical violation, or any act of malfeasance, misfeasance, or neglect of duty, on the part of any city employee, department, or contractor. — Price. 99